CHATS ON ANGLING

CHATS ON ANGLING

~

H. V. HART-DAVIS

WITH ILLUSTRATIONS BY THE AUTHOR

R·H·B

First published in Great Britain as *Chats on Angling,* by Horace Cox, London. in 1906
This edition published 2014 by Red Hand Books

RED HAND BOOKS
Old Bath Road, London SL3 0NS
1618 Yishan Road, Minhang District, 201103 Shanghai
150th Avenue, Springfield Gardens, 11413 New York
Şerifali Mahallesi, Umraniye 34775 Istanbul
Cross Road A, Andheri, 400093 Mumbai

www.rhbks.com

Sporting Classics No. 3

ISBN: 978-0-9575977-4-7 (Paperback)

Printed and bound in the United Kingdom.

DEDICATED
TO
THE LADY KATHERINE HARDY.

CONTENTS

LIST OF ILLUSTRATIONS

~

CHATS ON ANGLING

INTRODUCTORY

~

To those who love angling, with all its associations and surroundings, no apology may be needed for inflicting on them in book form certain short articles which have mainly appeared in the columns of the *Field*. They are "Chats" rather than didactic deliverances, and are offered in the belief that much will be forgiven to a brother angler, since all that pertains to the beloved pastime has some interest, and the experiences of the poorest writer that ever recorded his views and fancies may haply strike some responsive note.

But to the outside world, to those who care nought for all we hold so dear, to those who would rank all fishermen as fools, and would classify them as Dr. Johnson was said to have done—to such these notes cannot appeal; they will regard them, not unnaturally perhaps, as yet one more addition, of a desultory kind, to an already overladen subject.

No form of sport has so enduring a charm to its votaries as angling. Its praises have been sung for centuries, from Dame Julia Berners to the present day. Once an angler, always an angler; years roll by only to increase the fervour of our devotion. It is a quiet, simple, unassuming kind of madness, without any of the excitement or the glamour of the race meeting or of the hunting field, and the love and the madness are incomprehensible and inexplicable to those who neither share them nor know them.

The quiet stroll by the stream or river bank, the constant communing with nature, the watching of bird and insect life, appeal with irresistible force and power to the angler. As the short winter days draw out, and spring begins to assert her revivifying powers, the longing, intense as ever, comes over us, and we yearn for the river side. And the lessons that we learn from our love for it are not without value; patience and self-control come naturally to those who have the real angling instinct.

How widely spread this natural instinct is we may gather from observing the long lines of fishermen, each with his few feet of bank pegged out, engaged in some competition, and watching with intense interest for long hours the quiet float in front of him. Give him but a better chance of following up his instinct, and doubtless he would take with increased zeal to those higher branches of the sport that appeal more directly to most of us—the keenness is there, the opportunity alone is wanting.

Seeing that fishing and its charms have been so amply extolled and set forth by such able and various pens, from Father Walton, the merchant, prince of all writers on this subject, down to later days in continuous line, through such names as Kingsley (man of letters), or Sir Edward Grey (man of affairs)—writers whose works will live, and who can inspire in us the enthusiasm of sympathetic feeling—why, it may be asked, is it that we are not content, and that so many of us cannot refrain from publishing our impressions? There can be no answer to this query except it be as in my own case, the confession of a desire to record some of the experiences, gained through many years, in the hope that some crumb of information may be gleaned therefrom, and that the pleasure taken in recording them may find a responsive echo in some breast.

I would wish at once to disarm possible criticism by candidly admitting that this little work has no literary, or indeed any other pretensions. It is merely what it purports to be—a series of articles strung together, with the object that I have already described.

I would desire also to thank the proprietors of the *Field* for their permission to reprint such articles as have already appeared in that paper. My thanks are also due to my old friend Mr. W. Senior and to Mr. Sheringham for having been kind enough to glance through my MSS. and give me the benefit of their most valued criticism.

WARDLEY HALL, *August, 1905.*

CHAPTER I.

IN PRAISE OF THE DRY FLY

~

The methods of the "Dry Fly" Fisherman, as compared with those of his brother of the "Wet Fly," are absolutely distinct, and demand totally different characteristics. It is idle to compare them, or to praise one to the disparagement of the other. The sooner this kind of carping criticism is entirely abandoned the better. The dry fly purist may argue until he is black in the face; he will never convert the wet fly devotee. Nor, on the other hand, is there the slightest chance of the South Country chalk stream Angler being induced to give up his favourite form of sport. Quite apart from the fact that different waters require different treatment, the two methods appeal to absolutely different temperaments. Take for example the wet fly man. He wends his way, probably down stream, fishing all the fishable water before him, carefully searching with his flies all the quick water and stickles; placing his flies deftly near the eddy by that half-sunken rock, round which the swirl comes, forming a convenient resting-place for a goodly trout; or with careful underhand cast searches under the overhanging branches of yonder tree; always alert and on the move, leaving untried no likely holt, keeping as far as possible out of sight, and showing himself to be a master of his art. But he has always a roving commission. He may, of course, elect to fish up stream, and many an expert in that line may be met with; but, even then, his art differs radically from that of the angler with the floating fly.

From the latter are required in a special degree a quick and accurate eye, great delicacy and accuracy in the actual cast, and above all, a quiet, watchful disposition; he cannot whip the water on the chance of catching an unseen trout. His *rôle* is to scan the water, to watch the duns and ascertain their identity, to spot at once the dimple of a rising fish, and to differentiate between such a rise and the swirl made by a tailing fish. He will note the flow of the stream, and whether he will have to counteract the fateful drag. Having made up his mind, arranged his plan of action, and selected his fly, he will crawl up as near as may be desirable below his fish, taking care not to alarm in his approach any other that may lie between him and it; then, after one or two preliminary casts to regulate his distance, he will despatch his fly, to alight, as lightly as may be, some three or four inches above his fish. His field glasses will have told him, even if his natural eyesight could not, the quality of the fish he is trying for, and for good or evil his cast is made.

Perhaps he has under-estimated the distance, and if it be a bank fish he is attacking his fly may float down some twelve inches from the bank under which the fish is lying. In that case he will not withdraw it until it is well past the trout, but he may have noted that half-defined, but encouraging, movement which the trout made as the fly sailed past. His next cast is a better one, and, guided by the stream under the bank, the fly, jauntily cocking, an olive quill of the right size and shade, will pass over the trout's nose. A natural dun comes along abreast of his; will his poor imitation be taken in preference to the Simon pure? By the powers, it is! A confident upward tilt of the trout, a pink mouth opens, and the 000 hook is sucked in; one turn of the wrist, and he is hooked. Despite a mad dash up stream the bonnie two-pounder—in the lusty vigour of high condition—is soon controlled and steadied by the even strain of the ten-foot cane-built rod. Down stream now he rushes; he will soon exhaust himself at that game. Keep quietly below him, and keep the rod-point up. That was a narrow squeak! He nearly gained that weed-bank! Had he effected his purpose, nothing but hand-lining would have had the slightest chance of extricating him, but the rod strain being applied at the right moment and in the right direction, the gallant fish is turned back. That effort, happily counteracted, has beaten him; he soon begins to flop upon the surface and show evident signs of surrendering. The landing net is quietly disengaged and half submerged in the stream below him—for if he sees it he will be nerved to fresh efforts—and his head being kept up, he is guided without fuss into its embrace. And after he is given his instant and humane quietus with one tap, rightly placed, of the "Priest," the pipe is lit, tackle is adjusted, and there is leisure to admire the beautiful proportions of a newly caught trout, the glorious colouring of his spots and golden belly. Something has been accomplished, something done. A fair stalk has been rewarded, and it is no chance success.

Those happy days when there is a good rise of fly, when the fish are in their stations, heads up, and lying near the top of the water, and the wind is not too contrary, should indeed be gratefully remembered. A short length of water will suffice for the dry fly man—a few hundred yards. For him there need be no restless rushing from place to place. Quiet watching and waiting, constant observation of what is going on in the river beneath him, these are his requirements.

But on the days when the rise is scant and short, and the trout seem to be all glued to the bottom, or when a strong down stream wind nearly baffles the angler, then his patience will be somewhat sorely tested; even under these discouraging conditions there are places in the river unswept by wind, most rivers having a serpentine course; on one of these our angler will take up his position, and his patience and perseverance will be rewarded. And if the trout

WAITING FOR A RISE

be, as I have said, glued to the bed of the river, and there is no rise of fly to tempt them to the surface, he will wait patiently. It will not be always so; a change of temperature will come or some subtle atmospheric change about which we know so little, but which effects a wonderful change in the trout. They begin, as it were, at such changes to wake up from their lethargy, to come nearer to the surface and to re-assume their favourite positions—at the tail of yonder weed bank—or in the oily glide under the bank side. The first few flies of the hatch may be allowed to pass by them, apparently unheeded or unnoticed, but before long they settle down to feeding in a serious manner. Now is your opportunity, make the most of it; and if you keep well down and make no bungling cast, your creel will soon be somewhat weightier than it promised to be a short hour ago. Our friend the chalk stream trout will brook no bungling; he is easily put down and scared, and the delicate accuracy needed in securing him forms the most potent of the many charms of this most beautiful of sports.

Should, as may often prove to be the case, the unpropitious conditions continue without improvement, our angler is not without resource. His surroundings are so entirely congenial; he lies on the fresh green meadow-grass, the hedgerows ablaze with blossom, the copses in their newly-donned green mantles, blue with the shimmering sheen of countless blue-bells, are full of rejoicing and of promise. The birds, instinct with their love-making and nesting operations, are full of life; all nature seems to be vigorous with new-born hope. The true angler can rejoice with them all, sharing their pleasure and delight, drinking in pure draughts of ozone, and adding, perchance, to his store of knowledge of insect and animal life. His field glasses, as he lies prone and sheltered, bring him within touch and range of many sights that otherwise would have passed unnoticed. That water vole coasting along the bank side, pausing incontinently to sit up and look around, those rabbits playing near the burrow mouth, the moorhens cruising round the flags and sedges, all afford interest and instruction. In the very grass on which he lies he will find ample scope for observation and amusement in his enforced leisure should he care to watch the teeming multitudes of insects that throng it, his ears meanwhile being solaced and refreshed by countless woodland songsters.

CHAPTER II.
DRY FLY TACKLE AND EQUIPMENT
~

Modern glued-up cane rods have practically done away with hickory, blue gum, or other wooden rods—at any rate, as far as dry fly angling is concerned. Their action when well made is so true and quick, they pick up the line from the water in the way their forerunners never could; they are not liable to snap or break, and if tended carefully are very long-lived. Most of us have old favourite greenheart or other rods, companions in many a pleasant hour. We would not part with them, but on the other hand would leave them lying in their cases, taking out our cane rods in preference. The big grip on the butt, whether of cork, leather, or wood, prevents to a great extent the cramp to the fingers that would be certain to come from using our former small-butted rods in dry fly work.

Built-up cane rods vary, of course, greatly in quality and durability. Cheap ones may be bought, and they will certainly turn out a dear purchase. It is best to buy one from the very best makers only, and eschew as worthless all cheap imitations. Having decided to purchase a built-up rod, we have to consider its length, etc. It is, I think, generally agreed that a length of from 9 ft. 6 in. to 10 ft. 6 in. is ample—the latter, in my opinion, for choice. Messrs. Hardy, of Alnwick and London, have devoted so much labour and attention to built-up rods as to deserve a somewhat pre-eminent position amongst the many successful firms that make them. This firm produces many forms of rods suitable for dry fly work. Their "Perfection" rod is a very sweet weapon for the purpose, quick in its action, true as steel, has great power of recovery, and is light in the hand; but for choice I would pin my faith to one of their 10 ft. 6 in. "Pope" rods in two pieces. Such a one has been my constant companion for some seasons, and, though other makers may be able to turn out as good a rod, I feel convinced that none could turn out a better. The old attachments of the ferrules of former days have also gone by the board, and a bayonet joint has superseded them, to our great advantage. The upper ring on the point should be of the Bickerdyke pattern, the other rod rings of the ordinary snake pattern and made of German silver. The reel fittings should be of the "Universal" type, a conical socket taking one end of the reel base, the other end being secured by a loose ring. Personally, I do not care for a spear; I find them awkward at times, their only advantage being that your rod may be spiked when putting on a fly or when hand-lining a "weeded" fish. If one is desired, it should be carried inside the handle of the butt, the button screwing over it and holding it in its place.

I would not advocate a steel-centred rod, at any rate for a single-handed trout rod. The absolute union of metal and cane can never be secured, nor can the action of the two be precisely identical. Besides, how are you advantaged? The hexagonal form of the built-up rod is ideal for strength, and a rod without a steel centre can be made with perfect action, able to do all that may be required of it.

Reels also have undergone great improvements of late years. They are lighter, more easily cleaned, the check action is better regulated; a double check spring that allows the line to be reeled up quickly and easily, and at the same time offers a stronger resistance to an outward pull, is now almost universally employed. Aluminium, thin-brazed steel, have replaced brass and even ebonite. The air is admitted to the coils of line, and reeling up is rendered more rapid and effective. The "Moscrop" reel is excellent in many ways, and fulfils many of the chief requirements of modern reels, it has, moreover, a screw drag, which can be used to regulate the retarding action of the check. Messrs. Hardy produce an altogether admirable reel, which they have patented and call the "Perfect." Such a reel for an ordinary cane-built rod of the length we have chosen should be three inches in diameter, and will carry forty yards of tapered line, with some backing, if thought necessary or desirable.

Avoid for choice patent aluminium American reels. I have one by me whilst writing. The check action is outside, and can be taken off at pleasure and the line allowed to run freely without hindrance. The perforated face of the drum which carries the handle is counter-balanced, so that it may be used as a Nottingham reel. But the main advantage claimed is that the rim, within which the drum revolves freely, is springy, and by pressing the thumb upon it the drum is at once arrested and its revolution stopped. Of course, by this means your line can be absolutely stopped at any moment should a fish make a determined rush into any obstacle, but at the expense of your fly and cast. I am told that experts with this reel cast with a free line, arresting the fly at the precise moment required by the thumb pressure, and thereby assisting themselves in judging the length of the cast, and that the check is never clicked into action until the fish is hooked. I have often tried it, and found that the inadvertent pressure of the thumb or wrist upon the rim has cost me several good fish. In fixing your reel, I would counsel its being so placed that the handle is on the left side of the rod. In playing the fish it will be necessary, therefore, to reverse your rod; the line will then run near the rod and avoid the friction against the rings, and the strain will be taken off your rod, or, rather, applied in a contrary direction to that which it so constantly receives when casting.

The line should be tapered, and should be of oil-dressed silk, such as is now supplied by all good tackle makers. The taper should be five or six yards in length, and when in use, in order to obviate the constant shortening process it receives from attaching it to your cast, I invariably whip a length of stoutish grilse gut to its end, to which I attach my cast. This upper length can always be renewed at pleasure. This plan I find better than a loop. The weight of the line is a most important point; it should be as heavy in its centre part beyond the taper as will bring out the best casting powers of your rod. The balance of the line to the rod is all important; a little trouble in selecting a suitable line will be amply repaid. Do not forget, after using it, to draw off many coils of line to dry before finally putting your reel away, and, as it is important that your line should float well, do not forget to take some deer's fat with you with which to anoint it.

We next come to the cast. Two and a half yards of tapered gut are all that is necessary, tapered from stout to the finest undrawn procurable. I would discard drawn gut altogether, possibly because I am too clumsy to use it to my satisfaction. It is generally, however, easy to procure real undrawn gut of sufficient fineness from such firms as Ramsbottom, and a hank of such gut, in fifteen or sixteen-inch strands, should always be acquired when found. If kept out of the light, wrapped preferably in chamois leather, it will keep a long time. Take with you some dozen or so of such strands and a spare made-up cast in your damping box, and you will have all you will require in a day's fishing.

Your landing-net should be ample in circumference. The net itself deep and commodious; the ring should be solid, of bent wood, with a knuckle joint of gunmetal to attach it to the handle. The net should be of dressed cord, so that the fly will not become fixed in the knots. It is a great mistake to have too short a handle; you may have to reach far over sedges to get at your fish to land him. If you sling your landing-net on your left side, as is usually done, a long handle is very inconvenient in kneeling; therefore, use a telescope handle for choice. Wading trousers or stockings and brogues will complete your equipment, though, of course, some kind of basket or bag will be needed to enable you to carry your luncheon, your tackle, and your fish. All tackle makers will supply you with an ample assortment for choice in this matter. Possibly a waterproof bag with partitions and an outside net to place the fish in is the most convenient. Small linen bags in which to place the fish or linen cloths in which to wrap them are not out of place. One further article I should advise you to take with you, and that is a good pair of field glasses. They will multiply the pleasure of your stalk tenfold. With them you can search the water before you can spot effectively the most desirable fish, and ascertain more exactly what flies the fish are taking; whilst, if nothing is doing and the fish are lying like stones on the river bed or huddled away in the recesses of the weeds, you can amuse yourself with watching bird life and while away the time to your infinite pleasure.

Having fully equipped ourselves so far, we have now to consider our flies. I take it that no one who fishes with the floating fly nowadays clings to the use of flies mounted upon gut. Eyed flies have no doubt replaced them for all time. The very drying of your fly is too severe upon the heads of gut-mounted flies. Eyed hooks have, however, had to fight their way to the front, so prejudiced are we all, and I can picture to myself now a prominent legislator, a great angler and the author of one of the best sporting books published of late, standing by me on Test side, on a meadow near Longparish, his cap literally covered with artificial flies attached to strands of gut—a most extraordinary sight. The fish were most unkind, taking greedily some kind of small black insect, or fisherman's curse. We had offered them every kind of midge fly or black gnat we could think of, with scant success. Our friend, in gazing for the twentieth time at his fly-bedecked cap, saw a group of black ants, on gut, amongst others. The first one put on not only procured a rise, but hooked the fish; one run, and he was gone, the fly remaining in his mouth. So with the next. In vain we soaked the gut;

each fly met with the same result—it was at once taken and the fish was at once lost. The gut was absolutely rotten, and that pattern of ant was apparently the only medicine. Our friend fairly danced upon the bank in rage and disappointment. And it was all he could do to restrain himself from dancing on his rod and from using very unparliamentary language. I believe that even he is a convert to eyed flies now.

Whether the flies should have turned up or turned down eyes is a matter of controversy. Personally, I prefer the latter. In any case, the eye should not be too small, or much mental anguish will result. It is needless to say that they should be well tempered and with sound barbs. They should be tested in a piece of soft wood.

Have a reserve box of flies, made in compartments, so that you can replenish from time to time the little box you carry with you. This pocket box may be quite small. I like one three inches square and one inch deep, with rounded corners, and with bars of cork across it inside. It will carry all you need. My pliers I always attach to one of the buttons of my coat, as otherwise I am always misplacing them. Nothing beats Major Turle's Knot as an attachment of the gut collar to the fly.

If you should be fishing the evening rise at a time when it is difficult to thread the eye of a fly, even with the expenditure of many matches, do not forget before you go out to mount some sedges or large red quills upon fairly stout gut points and put them in your cap. They will come in most usefully, and save a strain upon your temper.

The use of deodorised mineral oil for anointing your flies has been greatly decried of late. I can only say that it is a great assistance, especially on a pouring wet day, and I should be sorry to be without it. I do not like, however, the inconvenient bottle generally carried for this purpose. I use a common metal matchbox, in which I have placed a piece of spungeo-piline, on which I have poured a few drops of the oil. The hackles of the fly can be pressed against this, and so anointed with the greatest ease. Fish do not appear to mind the appearance of the oil that, of course, appears to float round your fly; and, as they do not mind and it enables you better to keep your fly floating and cocked under adverse conditions, why not use it?

As to the flies to be used, as I have said in another chapter, the fewer the better.

CHAPTER III.

SOME DRY FLY MAXIMS

~

It would ill become a humble follower of the art to enter into a minute description of the various methods of casting, seeing that the subject has been so fully thrashed out by Mr. Halford, in his "Dry Fly Fishing"; mere repetition would be both wearisome and valueless. If anyone needs instruction on the subject, let him turn to that volume, and read, mark, and learn. It seems to me, however, that a correct style can best be obtained by accompanying and watching a really competent fisherman. No amount of book reading will secure this, and as in all kindred sports, practice, and intelligent practice, is absolutely necessary if the tyro would aspire to any excellence. The art of fishing the floating fly is not one that will admit of any mediocrity. It requires and demands such accuracy, such co-ordination of delicacy and strength, that mediocrity is impossible.

A few points may, however, be discussed with advantage. First, and foremost, do not be ambitious as to the length of line you can cast, or the amount of water you can cover. Be content, rather, to fish with just that length of line that you can control with ease and accuracy. In the actual act of casting never sway the body; keep the trunk rigidly still, never let your hand, in the backward cast, go beyond a vertical point above your shoulder; keeping the elbow near the side, get all the work you can out of the rod; it will do all that is required of it so long as you do not over-cast with it. Watch the expert angler; how easily he works his twenty yards of line; there is an entire absence of all effort; it looks as easy as shelling peas. The beginner or duffer will invariably put too much effort into his cast; he will not allow time for the line to extend itself behind him; he will bring his hand so far back that the fly will be hung up in the grasses or bushes behind him, and the force of his forward cast will make the line cut the water like a knife, and the fly will be delivered in the midst of a series of curls of gut, presenting anything but an attractive appearance to the fish. The movement of the hand in an accomplished fisherman is singularly slight; I doubt if it ever traverses much more than twelve inches from the vertical position.

Rest content with the ordinary overhead cast until you are an absolute master of it. When this desirable result is accomplished, there are one or two casts well deserving of care and attention. One in particular you should seek to accomplish—viz., the cast into the teeth of an adverse wind. Recollect that, under those circumstances, you can usually approach much nearer to fish than when the wind is up stream or non-existent; therefore you can use a shorter line. The cast is called the "downward" cast, and is really very simple. The backward part is the same as in ordinary casting, but in the forward delivery the hand traverses a much greater angle, and at the finish the rod point is near to the water. At the moment of delivery the elbow is brought up level with the shoulder, the thumb is depressed, the knuckles being kept uppermost. The resultant effect is that the line cuts straight into the wind, and is little affected by it. In a foul wind flies cock and float more easily than in a down stream wind; so this, at any rate, is in your favour. Yet one more style of casting should be practised. I have found it invaluable when awkward trees have been overhanging my own bank. It is what is called by salmon anglers the "Spey Cast." Inasmuch as it avoids the necessity of bringing your line behind you, its value is self-evident. This is the method of the cast: Having got out as much line as you think you will need, get it out up stream of you, bring the fly quickly towards you out of the water, allow the fly just to kiss the water when it is just level with you, the curve of the line being down stream of you, then, with a similar kind of action to that advocated for the downward cast, your line will be sent forward in a series of coils to the desired spot. It is always worth trying and may secure you a good fish, one perhaps that others have passed by as unapproachable, and which may thereby have acquired a confidence that may be misplaced. This form of casting is much easier in salmon fishing, as you are then fishing down stream, and the water extends and straightens your line for you. It is, however, quite easy of accomplishment, with a moderately short line, in up stream fishing.

Mr. Halford, in "Dry Fly Angling," p. 62, describes a cast which he terms the "Switch Cast," and it is one which, though difficult of acquisition, will accomplish the same object. He says, "It is accomplished by drawing the line towards you on the water, and throwing the fly with a kind of roll outwards on the water—in fact, a sort of downward cast; the possibility of making the cast depending upon the fly being in the water at the moment the rod point is brought down,"& c. Personally, I should prefer the Spey cast, and inasmuch as most salmon fishermen know something of that peculiar cast, I would urge its occasional use in dry fly work, more especially having regard to the fact that fish in such positions have acquired a confidence through never having been angled for, and therefore there is greater chance of a somewhat bungling presentment of the dry fly being overlooked. To describe the Spey cast accurately so as to convey the desired instruction in such a way that all who run may read, is not by any means easy; but, as I have before said, it is probably familiar to many anglers from salmon fishing experiences.

One more thing deserves to be borne in mind: always imagine that the plane of the water is some foot or so higher than it really is—that is to say, cast as if the fish, and the water in which it lies, were a foot higher than in reality. The result will be that your collar will fall as lightly as gossamer. One of the most proficient manipulators of the rod and line I have ever seen can pitch a fly, cocked and floating, almost anywhere within reasonable limits, but his line invariably cuts the water from point to fly, straight and accurate enough may be, but like whip-cord. Consequently, he is not the successful angler that his qualifications entitle him to be. An ordinary fisherman casting a less straight, but lighter, line will frequently beat him in catching fish. Our friend would beat most opponents in a casting tournament, but I would back many that I know against him in filling a creel.

Keep down out of sight, walk and crawl warily, and above all things avoid walking near the bank edge and unnecessarily scaring fish that others following you might otherwise have secured.

When trout are "bulging" (that is to say, as every angler knows, when they are taking the "nymphæ" just below the surface), it is almost hopeless to endeavour to secure them with a dry, floating fly. The fish are intent on another kind of game, and are best left severely alone.

Unfortunately, even experienced anglers are apt to be deceived by such a fish; the rise is often apparently that of a trout at a surface fly; a little careful observation will, however, convince you that such is not the case, for no floating flies are passing near him at the time of his rise. Don't waste another moment upon him, but try to find another in a more reasonable frame of mind. If all the fish on your stretch of water seem to be similarly occupied, and you are not willing to wait until they have decided to make a change of diet, then a gold ribbed hare's ear may, if fished wet, entice an odd fish, as it somewhat resembles a nympha.

It is, however, very chance work, as is that of endeavouring to secure a "tailing" fish with a down stream fly sunk below the surface, and jerked about in front of where his nose should be. No keen angler would call this serious fishing—it is a mere travesty of the real sport; but it may serve to pass the time, and perchance to wile a trout into your basket. The angler's patience will, however, be far more severely tried when fish are "smutting." What prophet is there who can tell us what we should do then? Those abominable "curses," so well named, appear to be able to baffle entirely the skill of the ablest of our entomologists, and the ability of our most capable of fly dressers. No lure has yet been discovered that can have any reasonable hope of imitating them. To watch a big trout slowly and majestically sail here and there on a still, hot day, barely dimpling the surface as he sucks down one after another of these little insignificant "curses," is quite enough to satisfy you as to the remoteness of your chance of deceiving him. Nothing that human hands could tie could simulate them. Place in the track of one of these fish the smallest gnat in your box, attached to the finest of undrawn gut, delivered with the lightest and truest cast of which the human hand is capable and, as you watch the fish fade slowly down into the depths in disgust at the evident deception, you will realise the hopelessness of your endeavour.

It is an old accusation against fishermen that they are apt to overload themselves with multitudinous flies, of which perhaps they never try half; and in this accusation there is a good deal of truth. I recollect one occasion in particular, when five men sallied forth to fish, and on their return all more or less bewailed the shyness of the trout, and each declared that, though he had tried many changes of fly, he had only found one to succeed. Oddly enough, each man had pitched on a different fly: they were the Driffield dun, the pale olive, the hare's ear and yellow, the ginger quill, and the red quill. In each case the size was similar, viz., 000; but the fact is, that most men have a favourite fly to which they pin their faith, and to which they give ten chances for one to the others. There are occasions, of course, where one fly and only one will succeed.

I well remember one day, on the Tichbourne water on the Itchen, when that fine stretch of water was simply alive with olives, coming in droves and batches over the fish, and when it seemed hopeless for one's poor imitation to succeed, even when put correctly cocked in front of a batch, or behind a drove, or by itself. The trout were rising slowly and methodically, letting many flies pass scatheless, but now and then picking out one without moving an inch from their position. I tried vainly to discover the method of their madness, and at last realised that they were selecting from amongst the myriads of toothsome *ephemeridæ* floating over their heads a redder-looking fly. I could not wade, I could not manage to get one with my landing net, so I put on at hazard a small red quill, with no response; then a Hawker's yellow got a rise or two, and even deluded a brace of fish into my creel, and then the glorious rise was over. Next morning, when whirling back to town, I found myself in a carriage with four or five anglers who had been fishing the next beat, and the murder was out. One fortunate man had ascertained that they were taking the ginger quills, which were very sparsely scattered amongst the olives, and that information resulted in his taking nine brace of beautiful fish.

But as a rule, it is far more a question of the correct delivery of the fly than anything else, provided the size be right. For myself, I never leave a rising fish that I have not scared, unless I am convinced there is some objectionable and unavoidable drag; sooner or later you will get him, possibly with the same fly that has been over his head a dozen or so of times.

We are all too ready to resort to a change of fly, and to leave a non-responsive fish in disgust, in the hope of finding an easier quarry. My advice is to stick to your fish unless, or until, he is scared. Possibly the most annoying fish is the one that drops slowly down, with his nose in close proximity to the fly, evidently uncertain as to whether or no it is the Simon Pure, until he gets perilously near to you. Even his scruples may be overcome if he gets back into position without being alarmed. One of the most successful anglers I ever knew on the upper Test, who owned a well-known stretch of water, was wont to sally forth with two rods put up, one of which he carried, while the other was carried by his keeper. On one was mounted a hare's ear, on the other a blue dun; and that these flies answered their purpose his records could testify.

A difficulty that presents itself to the chalk stream angler is the tendency of fish when hooked and when scared by seeing the angler to bury themselves in the heavy masses of weed. This has now been discounted by the modern method of hand lining—*i.e.*, spiking the rod and taking a good deal of slack line off the reel, and then holding the line in the hand and using a gentle pressure on the fish in the direction contrary to that in which he went. He usually responds very readily, and the rod may then be resumed. Indeed, it is astonishing how fish can be led and coaxed under this influence—the fact being that, the upward play of the rod always tending to lift the fish out of his own element and so drown him, he naturally plays hard to avoid this; take the upward strain off him and he becomes another creature.

Yet another difficulty encountered by the dry fly fisherman is caused by fish coming short. What angler is there who has not experienced this annoyance, and how often, as Mr. Halford in his work on Dry Fly Fishing has noticed, does the angler find that after the first rush is over and the hook comes away there is a small scale firmly fixed on the barb, showing that the fish has been foul-hooked? My observations on this class of rise would lead me to believe that the fish moved to the fly in the ordinary manner, but that something arose to excite his mistrust, and that he closed his mouth while the impetus of his rise broke the water, making the angler think that it was a real rise, so that he struck, and on his striking the hook took a light hold on the outside—a hold seldom effective, though most fishermen have landed fish hooked in such a way. I have generally found in such cases that a smaller hook has produced a more confident rise, and my experience would not lead me to endorse Mr. Halford's view that the use of a 000 hook handicaps the angler very heavily. It may do so with the heavy Houghton water fish, but I have not found it a severe handicap with the smaller trout—1 lb. to 2½ lb.—of the upper Test and similar waters.

A very keen and expert dry fly fisherman, the late Mr. Harry Maxwell, one of the best of friends and anglers, once showed me a method of taking fish lying with their tails against a wire fencing that crossed the Test at right-angles, the wire moreover being barbed. I was fishing in Hurstbourne Park, and he was accompanying me, as he often did, with his field-glass. Below the "cascade" a four or five-stranded barbed wire fence went straight across the water. Just above it, in mid-stream, in the stickle, a plump, transparent-looking Test fish of about 1½ lb. had taken up his position, and was boldly taking every dun within reach. My friend told me to catch him, and I said at once I did not know how to do it without getting hung up. He then explained his dodge, which may be carried out as follows:—Having waded in below the fish, take some loose coils of line off the reel in the left hand, then cast well above, and let the dry well-cocked fly float down to him. If he accepts it and comes down under the fence slack off the loose coils, get up to the fence as quickly as possible, pass the rod under and over, and then you are free to play the trout below you. If, on the other hand, he refuses the fly, do not attempt to recover the line in the usual manner or you will inevitably be hung up. Simply lower your rod point to the water, and then the quiet drag of the stream will bring your cast and fly slowly up and over the fence, even although the fly had floated a foot or two down-stream and under the wire. The action is so slow and even that there is no chance of being entangled in the wires, and as a fish in such a position thinks he is in possession of a vantage-point, and is seldom fished for, he is generally a bold feeder. Having explained the method, my friend made me try the cast myself, and the first fly floating near enough to tempt the fish was taken boldly; the whole manœuvre succeeded, and I was able to land my trout below me. Since then I have frequently made use of my experience, and with invariable success. If any anglers who are not aware of this method care to try the experiment they will see how sweetly the line travels over the fence without the slightest risk of entanglement.

There is but little doubt that the fly that is kept going catches most fish. On a seemingly hopeless day an odd fish here and there can be picked up if really sought for; and on these days the rise, if any, is so inconstant and so short-lived that it may easily be missed. On such a day, on the wide shallows of the Longparish water of the Test, three of us were struggling with the adverse conditions of a lowish river, a bright sun, and a great lack of duns. We had agreed to meet at luncheon at about 1 p.m. in the hut on the river's bank. I had found a seat upon the upturned stump of a tree in mid-stream. There were fish all round me in the shallows, but all on the bottom, apparently asleep. I knew that if I left my place and waded ashore I should move them all. I was enjoying my pipe, and so sat on. The whistles and calls from the hut passed unheeded, for I had noticed that my friends the trout showed more signs of animation. An olive or two came down, and gradually the fish seemed to rise from the bottom and take up their positions. More calls from the shore. I shouted back to them not to wait, and at length they gave me up as a bad job.

Soon a fish on my left front took an obvious olive, a pale one, and I had a pale olive on my cast. Still I waited, and soon the first few olives were followed by quite a little procession. I then cast over my fish, and at the first offer he took it. I got him down below me, and soon netted him out, wading up again most carefully and slowly to my seat; and from that position, in about twenty minutes, got seven fish in succession, all taken with the same fly and from the same spot. They were none of them very big, it is true, but they were all over a pound in weight. By this time my friends had finished their luncheon, and came out of the hut just as I was netting my seventh fish. Hastily getting their rods, they were just in time to get a fish apiece from the bankside, and the rise was over. Moreover, it was the only rise vouchsafed to us that morning or afternoon. So that the moral is that you can never tell when the psychological moment may arrive, and may easily miss it when it does come if you are lying on your back reading a novel, or with your eyes anywhere but on the water. One must lunch, no doubt, but it can generally be best enjoyed in the outer air, where you can watch the water and the fish whilst enjoying your luncheon and your rest. And on such inauspicious days do not relax your precautions in approaching the water, or from nonchalance or weariness allow yourself to cast carelessly. Your field glasses will often reveal to you a more likely fish—at the tail of the weed, maybe, or under the thorn bush on the opposite bank—and it may be worth while to float a fly over him and give him a trial. If he accepts the offer he is worth to you several got out under more favourable conditions.

When fish are really smutting, and the water is almost boiling with rises, the angler's patience is most sorely tried. Nothing seems to tempt them; the smallest gnats ever tied are far too big. Who will tell us what to do in such a case? In truth, I know not. All I can say is that they are in a peculiarly aggravating humour. How vexatious, too, are the tailing fish, boring their heads into the weeds and breaking the water with their broad tails—and their tails always look particularly broad at such times. I have at times caught them with a big alder, fished wet, and jerked past them when they have finished for the moment their diving operations, and their heads are up. It is chance work, and, if not productive of much use of the landing-net, will serve to pass the time and amuse you; for if you don't succeed in hooking many you will certainly get an occasional one to run at your fly, his back fin breaking the water and making as big a wave as if he were twice the size. In the quick water by the hatch holes on such a day you may find a rising fish, though when hooked he will probably prove unsizeable.

Never despair or give it up, unless you are one of the fortunate individuals who live by their water side, and who can therefore pick and choose. Where all days are yours it would be folly to persevere on really bad ones; but most of us are not so favourably situated, and we have to make the most of the odd chances we get. Therefore my counsel is to examine and watch the water, and be ever on the alert.

Where Sunday fishing is not permitted, the day of rest always seems to be the best angling day of the week, and you are tempted to be annoyed and objurgate Dame Fortune. Even then, if you are a wise man, you can turn such a day to your advantage by stalking up the water as carefully as if you were fishing, and by making mental notes that will very materially assist you on the following day. And if Sunday fishing is allowed, do not give umbrage to many of the parishioners going to church by making a parade of your waders and fishing rod. Either get to your water before church time or else wait till the church bells are over before you walk along the village street. Busy

City men get scant leisure for sport, and may fairly be excused for utilising their week-end holiday to the full. Much latitude may be allowed to them in this respect, provided they are careful not to outrage the religious feelings of others. A walk along the river bank, enjoying and drinking in to the full the beauties of Nature and of God's creation, may be as productive of good to yourself as an indifferent sermon. It depends upon your temperament and the power that the beauties of Nature have over your mind. They can preach as eloquent a sermon as was ever delivered from the pulpit, and may produce in you a frame of mind that may be of real and lasting benefit to you. No man should be judged hastily by narrow-minded bigots, or be termed a Sabbath-breaker for so acting.

CHAPTER IV.
EDUCATION OF THE SOUTH-COUNTRY TROUT

~

Surely angling with the dry fly can be claimed as the highest branch of the gentle craft? It cannot be doubted that those who have once experienced the fascination of "spotting" and stalking a well-fed and highly-educated south-country trout are bitten for life, and are, especially at first, rendered somewhat unappreciative of the sister art. The best fisherman is he who can best adapt himself to his environment and is ready to adopt the method most likely to be successful on the water he happens to be fishing. But undoubtedly dry-fishing labours under one serious disadvantage that does not affect the wet-fly fisherman, namely, the much dreaded drag, so sadly familiar to those who fish the rise with the floating fly. Who is there, however, who has not experienced legitimate pride and pleasure when, by change of position or by deft casting, its baleful effects have been overcome and discounted?

It is not given to everyone to command the sleight of hand of a master and to be able at will to pitch a fly, cocked and floating exactly right, whilst a bag of the line has been simultaneously sent up stream, so that for a short few moments whilst passing over the fateful spot the fly may float truly with the stream, out of the influence of the more rapid water between the fish and the fisherman. In streams where wading is allowed the fisherman has undoubtedly an advantage, as he can get more directly behind the fish, and so avoid the heavy current. But wading is not always feasible in waters such as those of the lower Test, where the depth of the stream precludes it. Even then, skill and local knowledge will often overcome the difficulty, and a fish in such a position usually falls a ready victim to the fly that floats truly, as he has been lulled into a sense of false security by his previous experience that dangerous flies leave a trailing mark behind them. But what a revelation it is of the education that trout have received, and how capable they are of absorbing and profiting by it! It seems almost as if the constant catching and destruction of the freest rising fish must be having effect in leaving those only to propagate their species which are either past masters in cunning or which are more coarsely organised fish, that devote their time and energies to bottom feeding and avoid surface feeding, except, possibly, at night; the universally acknowledged fact that fish are far more difficult to catch than they formerly were may thus be explained. Certainly, nowadays, an angler would be somewhat out of it who tried to emulate the far-famed Colonel Hawker, of Long Parish, and to catch the wily trout in that beautiful stretch of the Test while fishing off a horse's back. Nor could any modern angler hope or expect to approach the baskets that were formerly creeled. So is it everywhere. On the beautiful Driffield Beck, in Yorkshire, a paradise for the dry-fly angler, the club limit of ten brace of sizeable fish in one day used to be constantly attained, and that, too, with the wet fly up or even down stream. Now, with split cane rods, the finest gut, and the deftest of floating duns, five or six brace is about the best basket obtainable by experienced and most skilful anglers.

The natural question that perplexes and worries chalk-stream anglers is whether this "advanced" education of brook and river trout is to go on increasing. If we can only hope to catch half the amount of fish our progenitors did, what are the prospects of the next generation? Shall we have to fall back on black bass or rainbow trout to secure a race of free-rising fish? Or does the fault lie in over-cutting of weeds and bad river farming? I am inclined to think it does. Riverside mills are in an almost hopeless position commercially. The miller requires a heavier head of water than formerly, and with a decaying industry it is hard to refuse him, the result being that to maintain his head of water the weeds are ruthlessly and unscientifically cut over vast stretches of water, shallows are bared, and the holts or refuges of trout are done away with, and as a natural consequence trout become less confiding and far more easily alarmed. Modern agricultural drainage has, moreover, increased the difficulty by carrying off the water too rapidly. It behoves votaries of the gentle art to consider most carefully whether anything can be done to remedy the seriousness of the future outlook, and to disseminate the results of their inquiry; and if the Fly Fishers' Club, or some well-known leaders of repute, would take the matter up and tackle it seriously they would earn the blessings of the angling world.

It is considered to be undoubtedly a disadvantage in a club water to include one or two pre-eminently brilliant anglers, as it seems to breed a fear of their always being able to catch the easy fish, so that the more difficult ones only are left for the ordinary angler to attack. Not long ago I was invited to fish a certain well-known beat on the Itchen, but my host, in inviting me, said, "I don't know if it is much use, for So-and-So fishes our water, and has caught all the easy fish." This may be true in a sense, but favourite positions are always re-taken by other fish if the former occupant is killed. Just as a house in Grosvenor Square, or some well-known centre of fashion, will always secure a tenant, so a position where the trend of the current brings the flies quietly and steadily over a fish will never remain unoccupied. It is not so much the fish that is easy as his position, and therefore the ordinary duffer need never despond. One thing is certain—that the brilliant angler will never scare fish unnecessarily, and I would rather fish behind such an one than a so-called angler who, having successfully put his fish down by bad angling, proceeds to stand upright and possibly walk along the bankside close to the water's edge, scaring many a fish on his way up, utterly regardless of his brother anglers. Indeed, in this respect I think the etiquette of angling is hardly sufficiently considered in these modern days. Who is there that has not met, on club waters, the ardent and unsuccessful angler who wanders up and down, covering vast stretches of water, and effectually scaring many otherwise takeable fish, in the vain hope that he may find some purblind trout idiotic enough to take his proffered fly? I consider that unwritten etiquette demands that the utmost care should be taken by fishermen to do all in their power to prevent spoiling the sport of those who may be following. I can well recollect a day when the wind was foul, and there was one stretch of water sheltered on the windward side by a thick belt of trees, and in this stretch were located many heavy fish. Working up to that water, I found an ardent ignoramus doing "sentry-go" up and down the stream, walking on the very edge of the water. I presume he thought that if he only persevered he would eventually find the "fool of the family," but the result—the inevitable result—was that the fish were scared throughout that whole length for the rest of that day, as that stretch was bare and sadly lacking in shelter.

In considering the merits and demerits of dry-

Bringing Him Down to the Net

fly fishing, one cannot be altogether blind to the fact that down-stream fishing must inevitably prick and therefore educate many more fish than the floating fly. This being so, it is still more inexplicable that in former days, in chalk-stream waters, our forerunners were able to account for far heavier baskets of trout than we are, despite the heavy restocking our streams now receive, to their great advantage; and we necessarily come back to the old point, what can we do to secure an adequacy of free-rising fish? Is our system of fishing the rise wrong? Or does the mischief lie more in our river, water, and weed management? And can we so improve these as to obtain the desired results? Angling is now so much sought after, chalk-stream and other similar waters command such high rents, that surely it is worth the while of those interested in the sport to initiate and carry through some exhaustive inquiry into the subject.

CHAPTER V.
THE MAY FLY

~

The May fly is up! Every year, about the first week in June, telegrams to this effect are hurriedly despatched to those favoured few who own or rent water where this member of the *ephemeridæ* disports himself. It used to be called the May fly Carnival. There are, however, grave disadvantages in connection with our friend that greatly discount the apparent advantages. Fish gorged with this luscious food are wont to try a course of semi-starvation after their over-indulgence, and for a long time will not look at smaller and more wholesome diet. Then, to my thinking, a May fly is a horrible thing to cast with. It is not at all like casting with the more delicate duns or quill gnats. There is a clumsy feeling about it; it is exceedingly difficult to dry, and if you catch a fish a change of fly is at once necessary, the old chawed-up imitation being rendered useless. It is also not easy to get exactly the right pattern to suit, though for choice the small dark-winged May fly has given me the best results. It is, unless you live near your water, very difficult to hit off the precise day—you are always too early or too late; you are told "You should have been there yesterday; there was a grand rise of fly, and the fish were simply mad after them, and no one was on the water"—and so on. Cheery news, no doubt, when you find the fish all lying near the bottom. When they really are on, there is excitement enough; mad splashes all round you, frequently made by the smaller fish. Your proffered imitation may produce a rise or two, but somehow or other the fish don't take hold as you think they ought. You are inclined to lose your calmness of mental balance, to cast without sufficient care and with a half-dried fly. In desperation you put on a fair-sized red quill, fish more carefully, and probably get better results.

The main charm, however, lies in the fact that the advent of *Ephemera Danica* does bring up the big fish of the water in a way that no other fly food does or can. Hence its popularity, and in waters where the May fly is hatched in quantity, and there are heavy, big fish that as a rule find cannibalism pay better than duns, then the May fly has a real value. In other waters, however, were these big monsters taken out in order to secure a larger numerical stock of comparatively small but sizeable fish, I would have none of it; I would prefer to extend my angling season rather than take a large bulk of it condensed into one week of questionable pleasure.

Certainly, the May fly season comes at about the best time of the year to enjoy angling. A fine week about the commencement of June is most enjoyable on any river. All nature is at its best—leafy June, when sauntering by the riverside, even with scanty sport, is in itself a pleasure not to be despised.

Mr. Sidney Buxton, in his admirable "Fishing and Shooting," graphically describes a day in the Carnival time, when he grassed thirty fish from two pounds down, and of another when he creeled forty; but, good sportsman as he is, I rather fancy he would have enjoyed even more a day with half to a third of the basket when each fish had been stalked and picked out with a small fly. Not for a moment would I suggest or imply that equal care is not needed in casting with the May fly if you wish to fill your creel; but, all said and done, a bungling cast will often secure a good fish with that lure which would inevitably have put him down and scared him had he been feeding upon the ordinary flies. It is very noticeable nowadays how capricious the rise is. Indiscriminate weed cutting has almost entirely eradicated the May fly from some waters, and quite entirely on others—a boon to some minds, my own included, but a boon that bears sour fruit in other ways, for irregular and injudicious weed-cutting hits other fly food hard. It is curious, also, that in places where more judicious weed farming has been resorted to of late the May fly has begun to return, patchily and scantily enough, but nevertheless in increasing quantities every year. I would fain leave them to hatch out upon the Kennet and the Colne and similar waters, and leave our bonnie streams alone, but here there is no choice; if they come, they come, and we must make the best of them.

A big rise of May fly is indeed a wonderful sight, the drakes flopping into your face, covering everything, seeming almost like a plague of locusts. Fat, luscious insects, enjoying to the full their brief spell of winged life, after having spent months in the larval state. See that one floating down-stream, airing and drying his wings, floating on his nymphal envelope. He is floating dangerously near that trout that has already annexed a goodly number of his fellows. Will he be taken too? No; he flutters off, clumsily enough, making for the shore, only to be swallowed by a hungry chaffinch. So his brief period of air life is over. And what a feast he and his congeners provide for the swallows, the finches, and other birds. Towards sunset, males and females of the green drake tribe float and flutter about in the air, make love and pair, then the female deposits her eggs on the water, and at last both fall on the river with outspread wings, forming what we call the spent gnat.

The trout take heavy toll of the nymphæ rising upwards before they reach the water surface, and will not then look at a floating imitation; and when the act of reproduction is completed they feed greedily upon the empty shucks and the spent gnats. Altogether, our friend the May fly seems to spend a hazardous and somewhat inglorious life. Could he but see himself in his larval state, I feel sure he would lose his self-respect. He is then no beauty, and to grovel and lie low in the mud at the bed of the river for, as some say, two years, cannot form a very exciting kind of life; whilst if he escapes in the imago state, countless enemies lie in wait for him, and his very love-making costs him his life.

The return of the May fly to a certain well-known chalk stream in Yorkshire seems to be an accomplished fact, though one not altogether to the satisfaction of the members of the club that fish its waters. This stream, known as the Driffield Beck, ranks high amongst kindred waters, the dry fly reigns supreme, the stream is as swift and even, the water as crystal clear, and the trout as fully educated as those of their brothers of the Itchen or Test. In former times the May fly hatched in countless numbers on this stream, and the Carnival used in those days to be reserved strictly for the members of the club; but whether it were attributable to over-cutting of the weeds, or to some other cause, the May fly died away entirely from the stream, and for many a season not a fly was hatched. We members of the club—a very old one, by the way—rather congratulated ourselves on this change, as, instead of gorged fish who would not look at a dun for weeks after the May fly period, we were treated to an even rise at the small fly throughout all the angling months. But two seasons before we had noticed, to our surprise, the advent of a few May flies. I recollect impaling one upon a hook and drifting it down cunningly over a good 2½ lb. fish who had taken up his position under a thorn bush on my side of the river, and the scared bolt he made when it got to him and he had had a good look at it was a thing to remember. And, in fact, the few May flies which that year floated over fish in position made them all bolt as if they had been shot. Then in the next season there was a more considerable hatching of the fly, and in one spot in particular a few fish were taken with the green drake. The third year we arrived at the right time for the hatch, then a very local one on our stream; but in that particular part of the river there was a rise of May fly to satisfy the most gluttonous of those who love that form of angling. But the curious thing was the way in which the fish treated the fly. Every now and again the ½ lb. and ¾ lb. fish would take them boldly, and here and there a fish of that size would settle down to a regular feed, taking all within reach; but the heavier fish seemed to be thoroughly disinclined to take them. The bolder young ones now and again paid the penalty of their temerity, being consigned to the basket if fully 11 inches in length, or returned to the water if, as was too frequently the case, they were not sizeable. I do not pretend to any great experience of May fly fishing, though I have been a devoted dry-fly angler for many years; but I do not remember to have seen fish act so capriciously in my previous experiences. The birds, however—the warblers, chaffinches, &c.—were quite equal to the occasion, and took heavy toll of the *ephemeridæ*. I particularly noticed what I never remember to have seen before, *i.e.*, a cock blackbird darting out of the bushes at intervals to secure a fluttering *Ephemera Danica*, and returning to his shelter to pick the luscious morsel to pieces at his leisure.

My luck was not considerable; the rise of dun was insignificant, the wind was simply abhorrent, and my baskets, naturally, were not as heavy as I could have wished. The water was in perfect order, the fish abundant, but sport indifferent. One day I went up one of the upper feeding streams, where I had often, poor performer though I may be, secured a really good basket of good fish. After rising and pricking more than a dozen fish, all of which rose short, and turning over and getting a short run out of a three-pounder which had permanently taken up his position above a bridge by a garden-side under some sedges in a difficult position—rendered more difficult by the violence of the wind—I had to content myself with a poor brace of 1¼ pounders, going home feeling regretfully that I had done that day a good deal in the way of educating fish!

The last day of my visit (June 10) I had somewhat

of a more interesting experience. The wind was still high, though warmer, and, though no rain fell, there was a feeling that rain was not far off. The report that the May fly was up and in quantity had brought out a number of anglers, and when I got to the water-side, armed with a box of May flies given me by a prince among anglers, I found all the 'vantage spots (in the small extent of the water where the fly hatched in any quantity) duly occupied by an ardent angler ready for the fray. So I quietly gave that game up and retired to a small island between two branches of the river near the keeper's cottage. I had but a couple of hundred yards to fish, while the ground where I was standing was sedge covered elbow-high with charmingly and conveniently placed bushes here and there behind me, ready to hitch up any fly that, in the backward cast, should be driven by the wind into their embrace. The only chance was to keep up a kind of steeple cast, as the stream was a fair width across. The charm of the position, however, was that on the other side was a high bank with a plantation on it, which shed a welcome shade over the bank fish on that side. It was very difficult to locate a rise, but the stream was even and there was no drag. Nor was it an easy matter to land a fish, as the fringe of sedges was wide and thick, and the water deep; my landing-net was also over-short—a bad fault—and caused me to lose three good fish, one well over 2 lb. I spent nearly all the day on this place, and managed to hook every fish I saw rise, and that was not a great number, the rise of dun being so small and the wind blowing them off the river almost as soon as they started on their swim down-stream. However, I managed to land five fish, all on a 000 gold-ribbed hare's ear, the best one 1 lb. 9 oz. and the smallest a little over a pound; but as they were all in the pink of condition, and each fish was a problem to get, I enjoyed the day far more than a more prolific one, when the duns might be sailing steadily, the fish all in position, and where catching them would be far more of a certainty, and where even a duffer could not have failed to score.

Perhaps I may have been somewhat unfortunate in my May fly experiences, and most anglers would be disinclined to agree with my faint appreciation of this insect and of the sport he assists to produce. Most of my friends speak of this form of angling in a totally different strain, therefore, presumably, I must be wrong in my view. To me, however, the May fly (as a means to an end) is of great value in tempting up the bigger cannibal fish, but as an adjunct to sport, I am inclined to consider him overrated.

CHAPTER VI.
THE EVENING RISE

~

Having recorded my heterodox views about May fly fishing, I fear I shall run counter to the opinions of many if I venture to state my ideas relative to the evening rise. For my part I find it, in the main, vanity and vexation of spirit.

Doubtless, in the hot days of July and August, when rivers appear, under sultry conditions, to be almost tenantless, when after, say, 3 p.m., you may watch for all you are worth without seeing a dimple or a rise, it is some consolation to go home for a little rest and an early meal, intending to avail yourself of the evening chances with a possible brace or so of fish to save, maybe, coming in clean. Eyes tired with the glare of the water are grateful for the rest, and with the proverbial hope rising freely in the angler's bosom, you mentally reckon up the big captures you are going to make in the short time afforded by the evening rise.

Refreshed in mind and body, you regain your favourite spot at 7 or 7.30 p.m., and the evening seems to promise well. It does not look as if those cruel mists would begin to rise at sundown; there is little or no wind; the hatch of fly throughout the day has been insignificant; surely there must be a good rise this evening, everything seems to foreshadow it. You take up your station and watch the water carefully, especially the one or two spots near the opposite bank that you know full well ought to be occupied by good fish. A few spinners hatch out and dance merrily about; the gnats hover purposely up and down; an odd dun sails down ignored, as far as the fish are concerned, and at length, freeing himself from the water, gains the bank side. Surely that was a rising fish by the bank of rushes yonder? But the shadow of the rushes thrown by the lowered sun prevents you from locating him exactly. It was a floppy rise, probably caused by some small fish. Something must be done, for the time is short; so, letting out your line to the required length, you despatch your olive to sail down the bank of rushes. No response. Another trial provokes a rise, and you are fast in the fish; but, as anticipated, he proves to be a half-pounder, and, handling him gently, after having removed the fly, which was provokingly well fixed in his tongue, you carefully hold him in the water until he has regained his wind and recovered from his exhaustion. Whilst so engaged you hear a heavy splash to your right. Hastily glancing up, you cannot locate that rise either, but it is something that they are beginning. No sedges have appeared, so you retain your olive. A good quiet mid-stream boil above you attracts your attention. That fellow means business, anyhow. Your olive, however, though deftly offered, sails over his position unnoticed and despised. You change to a bigger fly, a 00 red quill; the light is still good. He refuses that equally, and whilst you are doubting whether to change or no, up he comes again. What is he taking? Some small fly, no doubt, but none that you can see. Try him with a hare's ear. You change, and whilst you are tying on the fly you hear a succession of floppy rises below you. You somewhat undecidedly give the trout one more chance, but half-heartedly, as you want to get down to those other fish—result, a bad cast, effectually putting down our friend.

The light is beginning to go, so you re-change to your bigger red quill and try your luck with those below you. Fly after fly, carefully placed, cocked and floating, produces but little result, one pounder succumbing. You see he is not a big one, and give him scant grace, meaning to get him into the net as soon as possible, and so bring him in half done. The net somewhat too hurriedly shown him produces an effort on his part, and he has weeded you. You spike your rod and try hand-lining; he does not seem to yield, and you are impatient, and resume your rod. Something must go; you have no time to lose. Suddenly with a wriggle he extricates himself from the weed, to your infinite astonishment, and he is then soon brought to book. But many precious minutes have been wasted; the fly has got itself fixed in one of the knots in your landing

THE SEDGE HOUR

net. Never mind, break it off; you must get to sterner business. So you take some few more minutes in threading the eye of a small, dark sedge fly, as the fish by now must be at work upon the larger flies. Flop! flop! on the opposite side, under the shadow of the reeds. See that your fly is dry and cocks well; keep out of sight—an absolute essential in evening fishing— and go for that uppermost fish. That was a good rise; was it at your fly? It is hard to see by the waning light. Evidently not. Try him again. This time he rises well, and you are fast in him; but you struck too heavily; he was a good fish, and you have left your fly in him, bad luck to it!

This time you have to make use of a match to enable you to thread the eye, but after some fumbling struggles you at last succeed. One more try. Pity you had not put on a somewhat stouter cast, but it is too late now. You must be a bit more gentle with them; a slight turn of the wrist is all you want. There is a good rise, just beyond mid-stream, and a good cast just four inches above the rise. You can see your fly, and also the neb of a good trout as he breaks the water to suck him in. Now gently does it! He is hooked, and goes careering up stream to the tune of the song of the reel. Steady him now; don't let him get into the rushes. The light is fast going, and you are inclined to hurry him. Better be cautious; his tail looked broad as he turned over that time; he is fat and in lusty condition, and has no intention of surrendering his life without a good struggle. Don't show him the net; that last run must have settled him; he flops on the surface; he is gently led into the mouth of the net, and is yours. Not so big as you fancied, by any means; might be 1½ lb.; you put him down as well over 2 lb. He is well hooked, and after taking the fly from his mouth you grip him well and give his head a good hard tap against the handle of your landing net; in so doing he slips from your grasp and nearly flops into the river. Hurriedly you put yourself between him and the water and get hold of him, making sure of him this time, and he goes into your bag. Is there still light for one more? Hardly, and it is no pleasure when you cannot see your fly.

You take up your rod again, and pass your hand down the line and cast. Where is that fly? Caught up somewhere in your struggles with the trout. It is engagingly fixed in your coat, about the small of your back. So you lay your rod down again, take off your coat, and extricate your fly with your knife at the cost of some of the cloth of your coat. Pack up your things and trudge home somewhat annoyed with yourself and thinking of the opportunities you had lost, and determining next evening to have some points of gut attached to suitable flies in your cap, ready for the fray—no more threading eyes under such adverse conditions for you.

Next evening you repair to the place where

you know the big trout lie and are sure to rise well. Fully equipped in every detail, and determined not to be induced to hurry, but to take things quietly and composedly, you reach your station. What is that in the meadow over there? A mist, by Jove! And soon the aforesaid mist begins to rise on the water, most effectually stopping all hope of sport; so reluctantly you leave the water side, a sadder and a wiser man, reflecting that the evening rise is by no means the certainty you had fondly hoped.

Of course it is not always so. I recollect one evening on the Test, when, after a hot day with scarce a semblance of a feeding fish, except tailers, there was a grand evening rise, and on a big red quill I got seven fish, almost from the same spot, in little over a quarter of an hour; but these days are too infrequent to alter my stated opinion that the evening rise is an overrated pleasure, and generally produces vexation of spirit.

If you do fish in the evening hours, recollect that you must be just as cautious in approaching fish as if it were broad daylight; that any sign of drag will as effectually put a fish down as in the earlier hours. Your fly must float and cock as jauntily as in the morning, but you lose the chief charm of fishing the floating fly, namely, that you cannot spot your fish in the water and watch their movements; you have to cast at a rise, or where you imagine a rise to have been. Use a small fly at first and then a little later change to a big red quill, or, if the sedge flies are out, to a small dark sedge. You can afford to have a point of stronger gut, for you will have often to play a fish pretty hard, and they don't appear to be so gut shy as the evening closes in. But as soon as you can no longer see your sedge fly on the water, reel up. Fishing in the dark is no true sport, and it is uncommonly near to poaching.

CHAPTER VII.

"JACK."

~

The upper waters of the Bourne and Test flow through Hurstbourne, Lord Portsmouth's beautiful park, and were tenanted until a few years ago by portly trout of aldermanic weight and size. It was found, however, that they proved too costly to be retained, as the toll they took of the smaller fish was prodigious, and out of proportion to their value. They were accordingly captured by degrees, and replaced by a more numerous colony of smaller fish. It used to be a grand sight to watch the big fellows lying in the quick water near the big stone bridge, or chasing the pounders with angry rushes.

When I knew the water, some ten or twelve years ago, there were still a few of these goodly-proportioned fish remaining. They were well-known, and each one had his nickname. Thus one was known as "Jack"; he almost invariably lay in a narrow outlet to a culvert that led the surplus water from the pool above under the roadway into the pool below the bridge. For the greater portion of its length the water ran underground, emerging from the culvert some two or three yards from the river. The ground on either side at the end of the culvert was fully three feet above the water, the banks being nearly vertical, while the stream at the culvert's mouth was only about a foot wide. In this narrow gully or channel lay Jack, his nose being only a few inches from the masonry. Any unwary footfall speedily dislodged him from his little bay into the main stream, but by crawling up warily he could be seen and admired.

Many had tried to secure him by fair fishing, but though once or twice hooked he had so far got off scot free. Nor was his post an easy one to attack; the water was, of course, gin-clear, very narrow, and also very shallow. The slightest sign of gut—and he was off.

On a lovely summer morning—to be accurate, the 26th of June, 1893—my dear old friend Harry Maxwell and I had fished up from the bee-hive, past the cascade, and were nearing the bridge with rather more than average success, and had decided to eat our luncheon on the bankside, under the friendly shade of the bridge. It was, however, barely half-past twelve— too early, we agreed, for lunch—so Maxwell went up a little to fish the shallow above, and I elected to have a try for Jack, as I had reconnoitred and found him to be occupying his accustomed corner. As the river was rather low, and as bright as only a chalk stream can be, I decided to break through my general rule and put on two lengths of the finest drawn gut, feeling that in this instance any natural gut, however fine, would be out of the question.

I was careful to draw the gut through a bunch of weed, to diminish the glare; the Whitchurch dun was on the water, and its counterfeit had already secured us some fair fish, but for some reason or other I was impelled to select a small 000 pale watery dun, called the Driffield dun, for my lure. After carefully testing my line and cast I waded out into the heavy stream, opposite to and commanding the outlet of Jack's bay.

Knowing that there was little hope of dropping my fly at the desired spot without giving my friend a glimpse of the gut, after a preliminary cast or two, to make sure of my distance, I sent off my fly on its errand, intending to pitch it on the grass just above the culvert. The first cast, fortunately, went right, and by a gentle tap or two on the butt of my rod I dislodged the fly from the grass, and it fluttered down airily in front of Master Jack, the fine gut never having touched the water. No sooner had it done so than Jack had it. Fortunately I did not strike too hard, as one is so liable to do under such circumstances; just the requisite turn of the wrist and the small hook went home.

Before I had time to realise fully what had happened the fish had bolted from his holt into the main stream, a bag of unavoidable line behind him as he charged straight towards me. On regaining touch with him I found that the hook had still firm hold, and that Jack was boring up for the bridge in the heavy water. Naturally, I had no idea of allowing him to thread his way up through the arch, as I could ill follow him there, so I had to keep up as steady and strong a strain as I dared. He soon had enough of that fun, and down he came at express speed past me, leaving me to get in my line by hand as best I could. By good luck, I was able to get the slack reeled up whilst Jack was careering about in the broader water below me. Hardly had I done so when, at the end of his run, he gave a grand leap, after the fashion of a sea trout; a dip of rod-point to his majesty saved a catastrophe, and I now began to try to reach terra firma. My friend, however, was not at all disposed to give me much time for such an operation, and just as I was trying to regain the bank—a sufficiently ticklish operation with a wild fish held only by the finest of drawn gut—he made a most determined rush for the big bed of flags below the bridge. Once let him attain that stronghold and I was fairly done; so I had once more to test my gut, and resolutely to determine that he should obey my will. Better be broke at once than lose him in that weed bed. Once more he gave way, and I was able to regain the bank. At that moment Maxwell turned up for luncheon, and the fish, now absolutely beaten, was successfully netted out. I found that in his mad rushes and gyrations he had managed to get two full turns of the gut round his gills. This no doubt accounted for his coming to bank so speedily.

He weighed just over 3¼ lb.—no great monster after all, you may ejaculate, but he was about the most perfect specimen of a trout I have ever seen, and was in the pink of condition. He now graces my study in a glass case, the only specimen of a fish that I have ever set up. But there was some justification for this temporary mental aberration, and I often now look at him and recall his sporting end, and the difficult conditions under which I managed to capture him. He carries back my mind to the fond recollections of my old friend, now no more, one of the best and most unselfish of anglers, whose untimely loss has left a blank among his many friends that cannot be filled.

CHAPTER VIII.
WEED CUTTING

~

A ll dry fly anglers owe a deep grudge to modern sub-soil drainage, which hurries, helter skelter, all the rain that falls into the river, thus doing away with the former gentle soakage into the soil, which served to feed our springs and keep up an even flow and an even head of water. Now we have but alternations of flood and emptiness; the millers, moreover, suffering from these alterations, and sadly lacking water in most seasons, cry out loudly against any obstacle in the river-bed; consequently the river weeds are ruthlessly and unscientifically cut away. The weeds, the natural nurseries of fish food, being thus reduced in quantity, the supply of food is seriously compromised, holts for the fish are destroyed, bare areas of river bed—on which moving one fish means possibly the moving of scores—afford neither refuge nor shelter, and become practically impossible to fish. All fish need shelter in the hot weather from the summer sun, all need refuges to which to resort if scared; take these away and the result must be deplorable.

Those amongst us who have had the privilege of fishing in waters where the cutting of the weeds has been scientifically and wisely performed will have realised the difference this point alone can make to a fishery. All the details of weed and water-farming have been so exhaustively treated by Mr. Halford in his various works on "Dry fly fishing," that they need not be described here. No better mentor could be chosen. But some of the chief points that ought to be had in mind may be touched upon. The chief desiderata, where there is an ample supply of weed, are, to put the matter very shortly, to cut in the deeper parts of the river lanes along both banks some ten feet wide, and in the shallower parts to cut bars or lanes across the water at right angles to the banks. At the same time lanes should, also, be cut parallel to the banks, to encourage the bank fish. Where weed is not in abundance recourse must be had to artificial shelters, or hides, under which the fish can obtain the shelter that they require. Stakes driven into the river bed soon attract a clinging mass of floating weed, the only drawback to their being used is that hooked fish may be lost through their bolting for and round them. Piles driven into the shallows afford a welcome rest to fish, and it will be found that a trout will nearly always take up his position behind them. Similarly, big stones placed in the shallows will have a beneficial effect.

The constant and irregular cutting of weeds has, moreover, a very trying effect both upon the sport and the temper of an angler. Huge masses of weed floating down, just at the moment when the hatch of fly, so patiently waited for, is in full swing, and the fish in the mood to take them, will sorely tax our powers of self-control. How often has such a state of things extracted from us a "swear word"! These very weeds may, nevertheless, be made to serve a useful purpose. There is a fine fish lying a yard or so from the opposite bank; the stream between us is heavy and quick; over the fish is an oily glide of water, the pace of the stream being checked by friction with the river bank. On this the duns float steadily, led by the stream into its embrace. Our friend the trout knows this full well, and therefore persistently takes up his station at that spot. We have often tried for him, but the pace of the stream between us, stand where we will, has always beaten us: no sooner has our well-cocked fly sailed into the head of the glide than it is hurried across it, leaving a most unnatural trail, or wake, behind it such as no living insect ever made. This trail of the serpent, or "drag" as it is called, is one of the greatest difficulties that we have to cope with in angling with the floating fly. It is, like the poor, always with us. But the very weeds we have been so persistently abusing may be brought into our service to overcome it. Watch a mass of floating weed that is about to be carried over the position of your fish, throw your fly so that the gut lies on the advancing weed; the fly, with some inches of free gut, should rest upon the water in front of the weed; the rest of your cast, being supported by the weed, will be freed from the drag of the stream, and the fly will float proudly over the fish. Unsuspecting he rises, sucks the fly down in absolute confidence, and at last he is yours. Backwaters may be overcome in a similar manner, and to this slight extent the curse of the floating masses of weed may be converted into a real boon. This slight advantage cannot be considered as counterbalancing the drawback of indiscriminate weed cutting, it is merely an attempt to turn to our use an otherwise unmitigated evil.

Proprietors of valuable fishing rights are strangely unappreciative of the advantages of scientific weed cutting and weed growing; they seem to be inclined to let matters take their course, and in consequence suffer considerably, and until they realise what this carelessness means to them things will be allowed to go on in the old groove.

CHAPTER IX.

THE ANGLER AND AMBIDEXTERITY

~

It has always been an enigma to me why, having been endowed by Providence with two hands, we should knowingly and deliberately minimise the boon. All ranks and conditions of men, be their occupations what they may, are affected. The nerves, sinews, and powers of our left hands are equally as efficient and valuable as those of our right hands; or, more strictly speaking, would be so if we only gave them half a chance. Who has not experienced the difficulty of folding a tie, tying a knot, or even buttoning a collar or a boot, &c., when the right hand has been temporarily incapacitated? And who, except the ambidextrous man, would be bold enough to shave himself entirely with the left hand? Injure a man's right hand, and you render him practically useless. Of all the arts, music alone trains both hands equally; in some trades, such as cotton weaving, spinning, &c., the left hands do their proper share of the work.

Consider for a moment the amount of wastage there is in manual work alone through this premeditated reduction of effective power! We seem to be content, apparently, to halve our powers, and this for no useful purpose whatever. The very children, who naturally would be ambidextrous, are chidden and checked by their parents if, following a natural instinct, they take up a pencil or a spoon in their left hands; and so on through their school days, and even after, each and every attempt to make a proper use of their left hand is sternly reproved, until at last the poor unused and untaught left hands and arms become of very secondary importance. Is there any phase of life in which ambidexterity would not be a factor of the greatest value? Would it not be a priceless boon equally to the soldier, the surgeon, the engineer, the craftsman, the clerk, or the artisan? And does not the same apply in the domain of sport? In shooting, would you not be at an advantage if you could shoot equally from either shoulder? The fisherman—how would it favour him? I unhesitatingly answer that it would aid him in every branch of his sport.

What angler amongst us could tie a Turle knot, or even thread an eyed fly, left-handed? We should fumble and fume, and probably give it up in despair. To the dry-fly fisherman the advantage that would accrue through equality of arms and hands would simply mean a duplication of effective power. Think of the countless occasions when an overhanging tree or obtrusive bush has rendered a right-hand cast difficult, if not impossible. In one position in particular a left-hand cast is of extreme value. It enables you to command the water under your own bank without having recourse to an awkward and always precarious back-handed cast.

You are carefully stalking your way up stream, the wind perhaps blowing towards your own bank, the left bank of the river. About twenty yards above you there is an overhanging tussock of grass with fringing blades hanging over the stream. Near this tussock, or a little above it, you note the dimple of a feeding trout; he is in a position where all the duns are brought quietly sailing past his vantage post. A well-cocked fly must inevitably secure him. You watch the duns one by one taken by him; he is feeding steadily, and seems to be a good fish. To reach him you have to cast with the right hand over the left shoulder. It is ten to one that, if the length of cast is correct, the fly will be guided, partly by the wind and partly by your arm, into the fringing grasses. If it can be snatched off without scaring your trout, well and good; but sooner or later, unless a particularly happy cast overcomes the difficulty, you are bound to be hung up in the aforesaid tussock so firmly as to necessitate a careful crawl to try and disengage your fly. If you can free the fly without scaring the trout, well, you are so far a lucky man. You either then recommence your struggle with adverse circumstances, or more probably give him up as a bad job. Use your left hand and arm, if you can, and the cast becomes a perfectly simple one. Every dry-fly angler, moreover, knows full well how soon constant casting and drying the fly tires and cramps the wrist and arm. What a relief, then, to rest your right hand and give your left a chance.

Nature has a wonderful recuperative power, and will reassert herself provided you allow her to do so. The reacquisition of normal left-hand dexterity is by no means difficult; a little assiduous practice, despite the first feeling of awkwardness, will soon encourage you to persevere. Practise on the lawn at a saucer, and in varying conditions of wind, before the season commences; you will not only gain additional interest in your casting, but will have acquired an asset of considerable value.

Not long ago, commenting upon what it was pleased to call the "latest craze," viz., ambidexterity, an evening paper made merry over the subject, and declared that there were enough awkward single-handed men in the world without seeking to add an army of still more awkward double-handed men. Such chaff may provoke a passing smile, but no chaff will ever detract one iota from the value of double-handedness, and I most strongly urge all anglers, old or young, to devote some little time and attention to the acquirement of this most useful, though so long neglected, bi-manual dexterity.

CHAPTER X.
LOCH FISHING

~

Loch fishing for trout is carried on for the most part amidst glorious and romantic scenery. There is a sense of repose in the drifting boat and the rhythmical cast. As a means of recreation and enjoyment it has a distinct place in the affections of many of its votaries, and that they are numbered by thousands the records of Loch Leven will amply testify. To the overworked man, to those who are debarred from active pedestrian exercise, this method of angling has a peculiar charm. To the thronging multitudes of big Scottish cities (such as Glasgow, for instance) the frequent competitions upon Loch Lomond or Loch Ard offer a change of scene and environment that is simply invaluable, whilst the ozone imbibed in such surroundings acts as an antidote to the smoke-laden air to which their lungs are ordinarily subjected.

But when all is said and done, to the ardent angler it forms but a monotonous kind of enjoyment. There is something so mechanical in the constant casting of your collar of three or four flies on the chance that some fish may take one of them. The row across the loch, the drift over the same ground, repeated constantly are apt to pall. Doubtless skill will assert itself in the long run, and every Scottish or Irish loch has its record breakers, men who can be relied upon to hold their own against all comers; but the novice and the bungler will often succeed where more experienced anglers fail. Perhaps the stream angler is too apt to work his flies to the top of the water, whilst the novice, perforce, lets them sink; and, as a rule, the deeper you sink your flies, within reason, and the less you play them, the better. There is yet one more drawback to loch fishing, and that is, that you are entirely at the mercy of the wind—or, rather, of the want of wind. A still, glassy surface, and your boat fisherman is done. May that not be because he is wedded to his three or four flies fished wet? Let him try a dry fly under such circumstances; not necessarily on the ordinary banks he is wont to fish so sedulously, but rather in the bays and creeks and shallowing water amongst the rushes.

On one occasion, about four years ago, I was in Perthshire, on the side of Loch Ard—that sweet loch, more beautiful in some respects than far-famed Loch Katrine. It was in early May. A big competition from busy Glasgow had put fourteen boats upon the loch, and some eight-and-twenty men were ready with double-handed and single-handed rods to measure their skill against each other. It was a lovely day, not a ripple upon the water. Ben Lomond's tops were reflected in the glassy mirror, so that it was hard to

A Dry Fly Day on Loch Ard

tell which was the original and which the mirrored counterfeit. For some hours these boats had, with precise and repeated regularity, drifted across the best ground without the semblance of a rise, only to be rowed round again to follow in the same procession. There is no doubt that their occupants were sternly in earnest, and would leave no chance untried. A faint catspaw of a ripple might secure a rise, or perchance a fish, but catspaws were few and far between. Hour after hour the rods were plied with stolid monotony, responseless and unnoticed. And, as the day wore on to noon, the conditions remained unvaried, and the catspaws even ceased to add a temporary and evanescent interest.

About that time—noon—I, having nothing in particular to do, took one of the gillies with me in a boat across the loch. He was astonished to see me take a rod, and no doubt put me down as a mad-brained Sassenach. Nevertheless I took my little cane-built Pope rod and a box of Test flies I happened to have with me, and we pulled up the loch and into one of the bays at the far end. There I bade him rest on his oars, as we were slowly drifting along the scanty rushes that grew out of the bed of the loch. I soon saw a fish or two move—at what I could not make out—so, taking an oar and gently using it as a paddle, I moved along until I could locate an exact rise, and I noticed a small fly near where the rise had been. Using the blade of my oar as a ladle I annexed the insect, and found it to be a small green beetle. In my box I found a small Coch-y-bondhu, which had a red tag and a peacock herl body. My scissors soon removed the red tag, and then I fancied it might do as a coarse representation of the Simon Pure. Having tied it on, I cast it dry at the ring of the next rise. It was instantly taken, and a plump ¾ lb. Loch Leven trout was soon in the net. And so it went on; a cast here or there at the rises amidst the rushes, and in a short hour and a quarter seven good trout had paid the penalty. We then rowed home for luncheon, and, on inquiry, I found afterwards that the united efforts of some twenty-eight men, all as keen as mustard, had produced three fish.

Does not this tell a tale of lost opportunities, and of the folly of being wedded to one style of angling? Had there been a good fresh breeze my dry fly would have been nowhere in competition with my eight-and-twenty friends. The best fisherman is the best all-round fisherman, able and willing to adapt himself to the circumstances in which he may be placed. But how little of this dry-fly work is tried upon our numerous lochs?—not a breath of wind, no good to fish! Yet ripples here and there are breaking the surface, showing that the fish are feeding.

Many pleasant half-hours have I had on the same loch, after dinner, under the rising moon, at the season when the main object of life is the grouse shooting. On a mid-August evening, after a hot day, the loch looks deliciously cool. Let us try our luck after dinner. We take our rods, and put up for choice a small gold-ribbed hare's ear. Let us get into that bay, in our boat, with our backs to the shelving shore and the moon before us. There is a good rise. Paddle gently, but quickly, near it; judge your distance accurately, keeping your eye on the very centre of the now expanded rings. You pitch it accurately, and it floats like a cork. Don't hurry to take it off—loch fish cruise about—he may see it. I thought so; a good rise and well hooked, and the pound Loch Leven fish merrily runs out your line. Now you've turned him. Don't let him get under the boat. He has run past you into the shadows, as that splash fully indicated. You can't see your line, nor where he is. Never mind, keep his head up, and, above all things, keep him away from the boat until he is done. He fights well, but the contest is a very one-sided one; he cannot beat you as his brother of the river often can, and in due course he is netted.

Now dry your fly well; or, better still, put on that other hare's ear you have already mounted upon a point of gut. We have rather disturbed this water; let us move a bit further up the bank. The rises are sadly infrequent, perhaps, but a brace of good fish taken under such circumstances is worth catching, especially as the loch is generally considered to be an early one, and the fishing to end in June for all practical purposes. If only you will try it, this floating fly work will add a very great interest to your enjoyment of your lovely loch.

Perhaps I may be treating this subject somewhat too cavalierly, and unduly emphasising my own views and predilections. Certainly I am free to admit that I have enjoyed many pleasant days on our Scottish lochs. One particular day stands out pre-eminently in my recollections. I was staying at a shooting lodge near Pitlochry, and the famous Loch Broom was within the precincts of our moor. To reach it we had a longish walk and stiff climb, as it lies on the far side of a high, saddle-backed line of hills. There were three boats on the loch, and one of them belonged to my host.

I was told that it was heavily stocked with good fish, but that a strong breeze was necessary if good results were to be obtained. In due course a gillie and I sallied forth one morning, somewhat late in the season, armed with rods, tackle, and flies, to see what Loch Broom would do for us. There certainly promised to be an ample supply of wind to start with, and, as the day wore on, it had no tendency whatever to go down, but rather to increase unduly; and when we reached the loch side after our six or seven mile walk, we found miniature foam-crested billows on its surface; in fact, rather more than we had bargained for. The boat had been merely grounded in the rushes at the loch side, and required baling out and adjusting. Intending to lose no time, I speedily put up my rod and my cast of three flies and placed it in the stern of the boat in order to soak the cast, then devoting my attention to the assistance of the gillie, who was getting the boat in readiness. Whilst I was doing so my reel began to screech, and I found I had hooked a good trout, my cast of flies having apparently been dancing over the wind-swept waves. It was certainly a good augury of what was to come. After a good deal of trouble we got our boat launched, and, though leaking a bit, it was in a floatable state. The wind was too high to admit of a slow drift across the little loch, but it did not much matter.

At every cast there were rises, not at one of the flies, but often at all three—no skill was required. The fish were rampant, and would be hooked. In fact, the main part of the fun lay in seeing how often one could land two fish hooked simultaneously. We only made three drifts in all, for it is easy to be surfeited with such sport. After our third drift was finished and the boat was hauled up again into its place we had leisure to count the slain; they were certainly very numerous. I somewhat reluctantly transcribe the entry in my fishing diary lest the tale may be set down as a "fisherman's story." They amounted in all to ninety-two, and weighed between 40 and 50 lb. It certainly was a record day for even that prolific loch. There is yet one more entry in the same fishing log to the effect that the 15 odd pounds weight of trout that I personally carried home that afternoon formed a considerable addition to the labour of the walk over the hills and against the gale, and that I frequently wished them at Jericho.

But you might go to Loch Broom on a still day and you would be almost inclined to declare that it was untenanted, so fickle in their behaviour are these selfsame trout.

There is a little loch—Loch Dhu—in Forfarshire, high up in the hollow of the hills, tenanted by many little black trout, who refuse to be beguiled by the artificial fly. I tried it once or twice whilst grouse shooting at Rottal, but with the poorest results. One day, very early in the morning, I was going up the hill with my rifle and glass in the hope of getting a stalk at a red deer before our grouse drive began. On my way up I passed within half to three-quarters of a mile of Loch Dhu, and happened to notice a strange turmoil on its usually unruffled surface. Bringing my glass to bear upon it, I discovered the cause. A swarm of bees was crossing the loch, a few inches above the surface, and apparently every one of the little black tenants of the water was engaged in gymnastic attempts to secure some of the bees by leaping bodily out of the water. The constant rising of the fish followed the swarm accurately across the loch, and only ceased when it reached terra firma. Then all again was silence and solitude. I certainly never tried afterwards to catch them with a solitary bee as a lure, and I fear that it would have required a whole swarm of artificial bees to arouse sufficiently the predatory instincts of these particular fish.

There exists in Perthshire, on Ben Venue side, snugly ensconced in a beautiful hollow below the lower tops, a lochan, or small loch, by name Loch Tinkler—why so called this deponent knoweth not. Round its heather-covered sides I have shot many a grouse, and enjoyed the great pleasure of watching favourite setters and pointers—those delightful companions of the now somewhat old-fashioned form of grouse shooting—point and back, with unfailing accuracy. Hither I have not infrequently resorted with my rod for an hour or so of fishing along its shores. The loch is very irregular in shape, and has frequent heather-clad promontories jutting out into its waters, which permit the angler to cover the fish more effectually, and seldom have I gone unrewarded. Of no great size or weight, a half-pounder being perhaps above the average, the Loch Leven trout that tenant it attain wonderful condition and brilliancy of colouring. They play well, and I should be more than ungrateful were I not to record the pleasant hours I have spent there. But, after all, a small loch such as this is, commanded as it is for all practical purposes from the shore, hardly falls under the category of loch fishing, a branch of angling which presupposes the use of a boat.

Owing, no doubt, to my peculiar temperament, I fear that I am not worthy of loch fishing proper. The thraldom of being confined for long periods in a boat, the unvarying monotony of the cast, are apt to pall upon me; and sooner or later, or, to be strictly accurate, sooner rather than later, I long to be ashore again, even though it be only to fish up a small Highland burn. And perhaps I am not quite alone in this respect, for I note that my friend who has given us those pleasant "Autumns in Argyleshire" asserts (p. 182) that he would prefer "indifferent sport in a river or burn to fishing the finest loch in the Highlands." So that if I err I do so in the very best of company.

And this same burn fishing has always had a charm for me. It is passing pleasant to wander with a small 9 ft. rod up the rocky bed, casting your fly into that miniature salmon pool or into that quaint stickle, whose larger stones shelter the little denizens of the stream, which, for their size, fight like little demons, sportive, hungry, diminutive specimens of the race that produces their bulky Test and Itchen brethren. One makes one's way over the rocky bed, under the birches and the rowan trees, watching the grouse, the black game, or maybe the roe deer silently creeping up, at peace with all the world, just as intent upon the capture of the little fellows as if they were salmon. The creel soon fills if the day be at all suitable. Their rocky home affords little enough of insect food, as their miniature forms testify; but look at them closely; how perfect their form, how beautiful their colouring.

A sandwich and a pipe give you all you require in the way of lunch; the whole day is your own, to do as you like with. Freed from all care, you are intent only on enjoying to the full the beauties of Nature that so lavishly surround you. Such quiet, gentle sport cannot but have a purifying and ennobling influence if you interpret aright all the beauty of creation. And it may be that interpretation is not needed; it is enough to *feel* that one has a place in so fair a world.

CHAPTER XI.

DAPPING FOR TROUT

~

This form of angling has been brought to a fine art in Ireland, and on many Irish loughs, in the May fly season, the heaviest trout are brought to book by means of the natural insect and the blow line. The columns of the Field newspaper testify every year to the efficacy of dapping, and, without doubt, many a heavy fish that otherwise would only live to prey upon its smaller brethren is thus accounted for.

We do not all of us have leisure or opportunity to test these Irish waters, or this particular form of sport with the blow line; but many of us come across deep, heavy runs of water, overhung with continuous branches, where the heavy trout lie, unapproachable and unvanquished, to become gross and even pike-like in the carnivorous and cannibalistic form of life.

Such fish are well worth catching, if you can get them, and far better out of the stream than in it. Wise in their own generation, they take up their holt in places where casting is impossible with an ordinary fly, and where, could you by any possibility get one out, your fly would remain almost immovable in the sluggish deeps and overhung holes. The problem is then presented to you as to how their capture can best be effected. This is your opportunity for trying dapping; and although, to my unorthodox mind, such fishing is parlously near akin to poaching, yet the accomplishment of their capture is so eminently desirable that the end fully justifies the means.

'Twas in the lower reaches of such a stream, not many miles from Bassenthwaite Water, that a certain number of leviathan cannibals had taken up their station. The stream was so tortuous and overhung that no boat could be manœuvred through it, and a carefully constructed raft, with anchor astern, had been tried and come to signal grief, pitching its unfortunate occupant unceremoniously into an unsolicited cold bath, from which he emerged with some difficulty. We then decided that it was impracticable for fishing purposes of the ordinary kind.

Walking home along this bush-covered length we could see the fish clearly in its waters, calculate their weight, and wonder how their natural fortifications could be sapped and overcome. We nicknamed all the fish, so constant and regular were they in their places. One, an ugly, ill-shapen fish, with a heavy head, was called "Bradlaugh"; another veteran, solemn and heavy, was dubbed "Gladstone"; a third, more dashing and combative, we christened "Randolph Churchill." There were about seven that we knew and named, and to the heaviest and thickest of all we gave the name of "Lord Salisbury."

It was a constant source of interest to us, in

going up and down the stream, to note what our named friends were doing and how they were faring. Notes were compared when we came in after fishing, and they gradually became an integral portion of our life and party. One evening I noticed "Randolph Churchill" greatly on the move, darting hither and thither in quest of some article of food. Peering through the bushes, I made out that he was taking something that was falling from the trees and bushes above, but what that something was I could not precisely make out. A poor bumble bee that had fallen into the stream was buzzing about, trying to free himself from his watery toils, and floating slowly over "Churchill"; the latter came up to look at the buzzer, and then bolted as if he had been shot. Evidently that disturbed even his equanimity. I had contemplated dapping with a palmer or Marlow buzz; and I sat down to cogitate. I called to mind the incident, referred to on page 50, of the bold rises of the trout in Loch Dhu at the swarm of bees crossing its surface. Whilst trying to reconcile their action with that of "Churchill" I was reclining on the grass, and happened to espy a green grasshopper. That might do, thought I, and rising, with the captured insect in my fingers, I again approached the water side. The bumble bee had most effectually scared "Randolph," so I walked down to where "Gladstone" had taken up his abode. Nipping the grasshopper with my fingers so as to kill it, I managed to flick it over the bushes towards my friend. It happened to light on the water at the proper place, and I had the pleasure of watching "Gladstone" sail slowly and majestically up to the floating insect, open a huge pink mouth, and swallow it. That was quite good enough for me, and after dinner I retailed to my friend my evening's experiences.

We were soon busily engaged in hunting up bare hooks and stiff rods. Fortunately for us there were some long cane-bottom fishing rods in the lodge, which evidently had been used in former times for bait fishing; the joints were indifferent, the whippings rotten, but the rods were, in the main, sound.

A little waxed thread and varnish soon put them into workable trim, and before going to bed we pledged a parting glass that some of our friends should gain a new experience on the morrow. And so it fell out. We knew that playing fish in such overgrown haunts was out of the question, and that if we had the luck to hook them it would be a question of pull devil, pull baker. Towards evening we met at our trysting-place. Green grasshoppers were numerous, so there was no lack of bait. As I anticipated, "Randolph Churchill's" inquisitiveness and audacity caused him to become our first victim. The bushes were far too thick to let us drop our bait near him in the ordinary manner. Our only chance was to roll the line round our rods, poke it through the bushes, unroll it carefully, dangle it before his nose, and then, if we had the luck to hook him, to give him no law, but to trust to our tackle and to hold on like grim death.

The next victim that evening was "Bradlaugh," a bold riser, who fought well, and who thoroughly justified his cognomen when on the bank. "Disraeli" was for some time our master; he knew a trick or two, and was by no means easily beguiled, though often pricked and once lightly hooked. Even his caution was at length overcome, and hardly an evening passed but that one or more of these, relatively speaking, monsters of some 2½ to 5 lb. in weight was landed.

"Lord Salisbury," however, proved to be a very difficult nut to crack, and beyond our powers of persuasion. He would solemnly inspect our lure, sniff round it, as it were, and then sink slowly down to his accustomed place. He seemed to know all about it, so, intent on other sport with the gun, we at last let him severely alone, telling the river keeper to get him out if he could.

One evening, as we were at dinner, there came a pressing message from the keeper to be allowed to see us; so, on ordering him in, a smiling rubicund visage appeared at the door, that of our friend the keeper, bearing in his hands a dish, on which reposed the vast proportions of "Lord Sallusberry," as he termed him, a tardy victim to the wiles of patience, combined with the reiterated attractions of a green grasshopper.

Possibly this kind of dapping may be deemed to be a poor kind of sport, and, speaking from a strictly orthodox point of view, the accusation cannot be denied. But, after all, it has its merits. It enables you, in waters where there are no May flies, to seduce the heavy fish into unwonted activity, and into taking surface flies. Thus you remove what are little short of pests in a trout stream, and you gain an interest in overcoming the difficulties of an otherwise impossible situation.

CHAPTER XII.
GRAYLING FISHING
~

G rayling have one advantage over trout in that they extend your fishing season by at least three months. Whereas trout may be called spring and summer fish, grayling are autumn and winter fish. While trout love positions under overhanging banks, or in the side runs by the bank side, grayling, on the other hand, generally occupy positions in mid-stream, lying near, or on, the bottom. In rivers that contain both fish, a bank rise may be generally put down to a trout. I would have substituted the word "confidently" for "generally," had not a very competent critic placed a marginal note to my MS., stating that "he would it were so."

I can well recall a day on lower Testwater when, in October, on a wild, squally day, with gusty rain, I was endeavouring to beguile some imprudent grayling into taking my fly. The river keeper accompanied me, and together we descried a nice dimpling rise against the far bank, above a plank bridge. I at once put it down as a trout, and was for leaving it alone; but my keeper friend would not have it so, and on persuasion I proffered the fish the fly that happened to be on my line. As luck would have it the fly pitched fairly accurately, and, nicely cocked, sailed down the bank side just where the rise had been. A confident rise produced an equally confident turn of the wrist; our friend was well hooked, and a merry five minutes we had before he could be beguiled into the landing net. He proved to be a fine trout, over 3 lb. in weight and in magnificent condition, but the month was against us, and we had to replace him with all due care in his native element before resuming our search for the grayling, who were not at all inclined to favour us, on that occasion at any rate.

This particular fish certainly endorsed my view, for I felt confident in my first opinion, viz., that it was the rise of a trout, and not that of a grayling. The keeper, however, was equally confident until he was proved wrong, and, as his experiences were a hundredfold greater than mine, I would certainly not attempt to advance my own as against his. It is so terribly easy to generalise from inadequate experience.

One thing I certainly have learned with regard to grayling fishing with a hackle fly, fished wet and up stream, and that is, how easily one may miss them through want of rapidity in the strike. I remember a friend of mine dancing with laughter on the river bank as he watched me miss rise after rise under such circumstances. I seemed to be always a little after the fair. It was blind kind of work, casting at the rises, the fish having to come up from the bottom to the fly, and somehow or other they seemed always to take the wrong psychological moment for their rise as far as I was concerned. Occasionally, of course, I hooked what I fancied to be a silly idiot of a fish, and it was not until my friend had a turn at them and then declared they were rising disgracefully short that I was able to turn the laugh against him. When I was angling it was always the fault of the angler that the fish were not hooked; when his turn came it was entirely the fault of the fish. At the same time it is undeniable that to secure grayling, especially heavy ones, by this manner of angling requires great alertness, and, as it were, sympathy of touch in hooking them.

I cannot pretend to any considerable experiences in grayling fishing, but I do not agree with Mr. G. A. B. Dewar, who, in his "Book of the Dry Fly," p. 54 (Lawrence & Bullen, 1897), states confidently that angling for the grayling with the dry fly is "poor fun." On the contrary, I have found him a bold riser, and a really free fighter in his own style. He will take a dry fly in hot, bright weather, though his real value comes in on frosty days, after the trout have earned their well-deserved rest from the plague of artificial flies. A grayling, moreover, is in his element in deep pools and quiet hollows, where one would hardly expect to see the dimple of a rising trout. At the same time the fish loves rapid streams and shallows, retiring for rest to the deeper pools.

To be absolutely candid, I would always prefer to fish for trout rather than to fish for grayling. This may possibly be through lack of experience and opportunity; but no one can gainsay the fact that grayling are in condition when trout are not, that they are a worthy quarry and gamesome, despite (Brother) Cotton's condemnation of them as "dead-hearted" fish. To be able to defer putting away one's favourite

LUNCHEON

rods until October, November, and even December have passed away is no mean advantage, and I, for one, would be indeed sorry to decry the grayling in any way whatever.

Grayling do not, as a rule, rise as freely as trout will do during heavy rain, nor does muggy weather suit them; the best time for grayling fishing in late autumn or early winter is from about twelve to two, on a bright day, after a sharp and crisp frost. As they lie so low in the water and have to come to the surface to take a fly, they frequently miss their object, whether real or artificial; and after they have taken the fly, or missed it, as the case may be, they dive downwards to the bottom again, often breaking the water with their forked tails in so doing. They are, therefore, more easy of approach than trout, as there is a larger intervening amount of water to screen you. As they take surface food, and yet lie so deep, their quaint lozenge-shaped eyes have an upward turn. They are peculiarly gut shy, and any undue coarseness in this respect or glistening glare in your cast will effectually choke them off from their intended rise. They may be taken by almost any of the ordinary surface flies, by a red tag, or by means of many of the pale watery hackle flies fished wet. The depth of the water in which they love to lie renders them less susceptible to continued flogging than trout. Remember, if you hook a good grayling, that the corners of his mouth are very tender compared with those of a trout, and that, salmon-like, he takes a header downwards after taking your fly, thus tending to hook himself; therefore the quickest and gentlest of wrist turns is sufficient to cement the attachment between you. And although grayling fishermen will not admit that the mouth of a grayling is more tender, generally speaking, than that of a trout, it is extraordinary how often the fly happens to attach itself to those particularly tender spots. In playing him, this fact should not be forgotten, nor the fact that the appearance of the landing net seems to produce in him the wildest and most frantic efforts for freedom.

Grayling receive universal condemnation for poaching trout and salmon ova, and it is only right to own that they are grave delinquents in this respect. The unfortunate ova have, however, a multitude of enemies in the shape of various water birds, ducks, swans, &c., and the toll taken by the grayling in proportion cannot be so very heavy after all, or they would not be permitted to continue to populate our south country streams, where the trout is the chief object of worship. At any rate, they have no other cannibal proclivities, which is more than can be said for the noble trout himself, who is a marked sinner in both respects.

Grayling will not thrive in all streams; they love alternate shallows and deeps, and are particularly partial to quiet backwaters. They are very migratory, and will frequently shift their quarters. The character of the river appears to be all-important in their case, and many streams suitable for trout will not hold grayling. But where the surrounding circumstances are suitable, and the temperature of the water is neither too cold nor too hot, it seems a pity that they should not be given a trial. They spawn in April, and recover their condition more rapidly than trout. I do not know whether the origin of these fish in British waters has ever been ascertained. They may have been brought to these islands by the monks in former time, who so carefully husbanded all resources in the shape of fish food; but I have never seen or read any authentic statement to this effect, and would prefer to consider them as indigenous.

CHAPTER XIII.
NOTES ON RAINBOW TROUT
~

Rainbows are a comparatively recent importation into our native waters, and appeared just at the time when they were most needed. It is but a few years since our British waters, neglected, except in a few instances, began to receive the attention they deserved, in view of their intrinsic value. Steps were then taken to diminish, if not entirely to remove, the terribly universal pollution of our streams and rivers. From that time trout fishing prospects in river and stream began to look up and improve; but our ponds and reservoirs, if stocked with fish at all, contained only the coarse fish of former times. By a happy coincidence the rainbow trout, which we owe to our cousins of the United States, began to be talked about and known. Speedily our fish-culturists took them up and established them in their hatcheries, with the best results. A more sporting or gamer fish does not exist. He rises most freely to the fly—up to a certain weight—and, when hooked, plays as gamely as any sea trout. He grows with astonishing rapidity. In our local waters, two-year-old fish, 8 in. long in February, have grown to ¾ lb. fish and even to pounders in September. There is therefore no excuse for leaving our ponds untenanted by these gamesome fish. Moreover, their edible qualities are quite first-rate; they are shapely, beautiful in colouring, and thrive in any kind of water. One point, however, should be carefully guarded against. Rainbows are great travellers; they will push up, especially before spawning, and it is therefore necessary to confine them by a grid at the head and foot of your water.

The spawning time for these fish in their natural habitat is rather late in the spring; but, as might be expected from analogy, rainbows bred and reared in this country appear to be adapting themselves to their environment, and to be gradually assimilating their time for spawning to that of our local trout. The bulk of rainbows spawn in British waters about February and March, many retain their old times of May and June, whilst a proportion have adapted themselves to their surroundings and spawn as early as brook trout. I think that the date is more or less influenced by the amount of fish food obtainable. Thus, for instance, with hand-fed fish the old later dates are maintained; but it is still doubtful, as far as my experience goes, as to whether the ova of the fish that are dependent entirely upon natural food is ever vivified. My fish undoubtedly have spawned on the prepared beds, but, so far, I have not been able to establish any evidence of matured fry. The edges of the water this summer were filled with multitudinous small fry no doubt, but on careful inspection they proved to be entirely the fry of sticklebacks, perch, &c. I have found hen fish gravid with ova as early as November and as late as April. In time, no doubt, their spawning season will coincide with that of our brown trout. And herein lies a field for investigation and careful watching. It is held in many quarters that rainbows do not breed in Great Britain. My experience hardly tallies with this belief. On our waters in Lancashire, where we had no gravel beds suitable for the deposit of ova, I found late last year several hen fish, of from 1½ lb. to 2 lb. in weight, dead in the water; they were full of ripe ova, and had undoubtedly died through being egg-bound. I then made some spawning redds suitable for the deposit and fertilisation of the ova, and it has been highly interesting to see the fish elbowing each other to secure a spot for themselves. Since then I have caught many spent fish, both cock and hen, showing that the ova, at any rate, have been duly deposited; but so far I have not been able to identify the fry. A large quantity of fry of sorts I have secured this season, but they proved to be the fry of stickleback. The "Trinity" two-year-old fish I restocked with seem to be growing admirably. This form of rainbow trout have the reputation of being, if possible, freer risers, quicker growers, and harder fighters than the ordinary kind; so far they seem to act up to their reputation. The few I have caught fought like little demons, and it was almost difficult to be able to restore them to the water and free the hook before they had been practically exhausted by their frantic efforts for freedom.

The proper amount of fish with which to stock a given area of water depends several circumstances. First and foremost, of course, it depends upon the amount of fish food in it. Many pools and ponds are full of fresh-water shrimps, snails, and the like, all of which are of very great value in developing and fattening your fish. But as you do not want to depend upon bottom feeding for their whole stock of food, admirable adjunct though it may be, it is well to place round the margins of your waters all plants that encourage the increase of fly food. Beds of the ordinary watercress are not only valuable in this respect, but afford welcome shelter. Water lilies, if kept within bounds, are equally valuable, and it must never be forgotten that, especially in shallow water, shelter from the summer sun is an absolute necessity if you wish your stock to improve. Other aquatic and semi-aquatic plants should also be utilised freely, such as marsh marigolds, starworts, bulrushes, &c. Nor should it be forgotten to plant alders and fringing willows here and there. All trout, particularly rainbows, take an alder fly readily.

A certain area of water will not support more than a certain weight of fish life. You can therefore either have that weight made up by a large quantity of small fish or by a correspondingly smaller number of larger fish. It is not prudent, therefore, to overstock. This question has necessarily very considerable bearing upon your calculations. Nor is it possible to fix arbitrarily any precise number of fish as being capable of being supported by a given area of water; an examination of the water itself would be needed to determine this with any degree of accuracy.

Having, however, once determined upon the proper stock required—and, in my opinion, it pays better to stock with two-year-old fish than with yearlings—then an accurate account should be kept of the fish taken out of the water each season, and a corresponding number should be turned in each November for restocking, a few being added for contingencies.

As I have already stated, when rainbows grow into really big fish—say over 2½ lb.—they appear, in our British waters, to develop lazy, bottom-feeding proclivities. It will be necessary, therefore, or at any rate advisable, to take these fish out by using a bright salmon fly, fished deep, or a minnow, fished as deep as the water will admit. When the fish are first placed in their fresh home it is customary to feed them with artificial food until they get accustomed to their surroundings. For this purpose liver is often used, and it is quite an amusing sight to see them "boil" when such food is distributed. It is very doubtful whether it is wise to feed with such fat-producing foods.

Some authorities hold that fatty foods of any kind produce disease of the liver and fatty degeneration, and condemn absolutely all red meat. If this be so— and it appears to be not only probable, but proved by expert experience—it is better to let the fish take care of themselves and eschew all kinds of artificial food stuffs.

When stocking, every care should be taken to see that when the fish arrive they are placed as soon as possible where the water is most lively and broken, so that they may, at the earliest practicable moment, obtain the air they so much need after their journey. The water in the cans should never be allowed to stagnate. One more precaution is indispensable, viz., to see, by means of a thermometer, that the temperature of the water in the stream or pond is the same as that in the cans. If there should be any difference—and there will almost certainly be—it can easily be adjusted by letting some water out of the cans and substituting that of the stream. By doing this gradually the fish will become acclimatised to the change. The cans on the cart, meanwhile, should be agitated, and therefore aerated, by keeping the cart on the move. Neglect of this will cause serious risk of loss. Once safely deposited in their new home, the fish will speedily spread over your whole water, even if all were put in at one spot. Perhaps it is unnecessary to add that fish should never be handled when being put into the water. A small flat net will pick up any that may have fallen on the ground during the change of water. It is surprising how thoughtless many people are about handling and treating fish. Thus, for instance, if an undersized fish is caught it is, in common parlance, "thrown back," and is often in reality so treated. Too much care cannot be taken in replacing fish. If put back gently and held for a few seconds in a proper position, back up, they will soon recover from their exhaustion and glide away unharmed; whereas, if "thrown in," or dropped in in a careless manner, they will turn belly up, and probably never recover.

When all precautions are taken, and your waters have been intelligently treated, and suitable spawning redds are provided, you will never regret having stocked with rainbows, for the sport you will obtain from them will more than amply repay you for the trouble you may have taken.

CHAPTER XIV.
SALMON FISHING
~

Formerly, and indeed not so very long ago, no one in the Highlands of Scotland was considered free of the hill, or indeed of any account, unless and until he had slain a stag, a salmon, and an eagle. Nowadays, matters are somewhat different. The two former, inhabiting as they do the forests and rivers, are in great request, and have a considerable money value, and, in consequence, have passed into the hands of those who have the deepest purses, saving and except where some few Highland lairds and noblemen retain their ancient rights in their own hands, and dispense their hospitality amongst their friends as of yore. As for the golden eagle, few would attempt, or even wish, to shoot so noble a bird. The ordinary forest fine of £500 is a sufficient deterrent, if, indeed, any is necessary. Every effort is now being made, and should be made, to keep the (now, alas! scarce) king of the birds amongst us.

But if, as we have said, the large majority of the forests and salmon rivers are rented by those who are able and willing to pay almost any price for the dignity of being lessees of such tempting and highly-prized sporting grounds, the general appetite and desire have developed and grown enormously. Ever-increasing facilities for travelling have brought with them an ever-growing army of men, all eager to get good salmon fishing, and searching high and low to secure it. Norway, Sweden, Iceland, Canada, British Columbia, and a host of other portions of the globe have been brought into requisition in order to satisfy some portion of this craving. Small wonder, then, that rents for rivers, spring or autumn, continue to increase, and that the Government of the day is being constantly and consistently urged to increase the close time for net fishing, in order that the upper riparian owners may have some chance of replenishing their pools.

A man who has once hooked and played a clean-run salmon, and has experienced the thrill of excitement that continues from the rise until the salmon is safely landed, is not at all likely to forget it, or to miss any chance of renewing his acquaintance with *Salmo salar*.

The contest is such a fair one, there are so many chances in favour of the fish, that no element of sport is wanting. He is so strong in the water, so perfectly built for speed, that unless you handle him both carefully and skilfully you may easily lose him, even if you have brought him exhausted to the gaff. In that perilous moment, when flopping and surging near the top of the water, how many a fish effects his escape! And who is there amongst us but has experienced the sickening feeling of the straightened rod, and the fly released from the worn hold in the fish's mouth? It is just the uncertainty of the sport, added to the strength and vigour of a hooked fish, that form the great allurement to salmon anglers.

Whilst in trout fishing—more especially with the dry fly—great accuracy and delicacy of cast are required, the actual fishing for salmon with the fly makes no such demands upon the angler. Provided that he can throw a tolerably straight line of reasonable length, so as to cover the places in the pools where the salmon are wont to rise, many faults that would entail failure with the dry fly will pass unnoticed, owing to the fly having been cast into swiftly running water, which brawling water straightens out in the kindest manner the kinks formed in the line by the incompetency of the wielder of the rod.

To this extent, therefore, a novice may have the good fortune to beat the more experienced hand. Once hooked, however, the novice is out of it, unless he has at hand an experienced mentor, and the odds are largely in favour of the fish. It is then that the accomplished angler asserts himself. I have heard of men who consider that the excitement of salmon fishing begins and ends with the hooking of the fish, who are willing to hand over to their attendant, or gillie, the duty which they consider to be monotonous and fatiguing—of playing the fish.

For my part, I look at the matter from an entirely different point of view. The combat between the fisherman and the fish is essentially a gallant one. In the water, a clean-run fish of, say, 18 lb. really plays the angler for some space of time, and you recognise that although your experience and intelligence may enable you, within a reasonable time, to be the victor, yet that you have attached to you a quarry well worthy of your skill, and one, moreover, who may yet call forth all your activity and resource, and who cannot be accounted as caught until he is absolutely on the grass beside you.

I, on the contrary, always consider that playing a salmon is the most exciting and interesting part of the sport. In playing a fish, whether it be a heavy trout on a light, single-handed rod, or a clean-run active salmon on a proportionately suitable rod, a sense of touch is needed that bears some resemblance to that necessary for the proper handling of the reins in riding a keen young thoroughbred horse. You require a keen appreciation of when to allow a certain latitude and when to exercise all the pressure that the occasion demands.

A heavy-handed man will soon render a sensitive-mouthed young horse half demented, whilst at the same time quiet, strong hands exert just that influence that is needed to control his vagaries. Some men are born with the requisite sensitiveness of touch, others will be clumsy and heavy-handed to the end of their days. Some will give undue licence to a fish, will allow him to play for an inordinate length of time, triplicating thereby the risk of losing him.

It is not possible to lay down on paper any regulations for playing fish beyond what may be termed the "A B C" of the game. You should never allow your rod point to be dragged down below an angle of 45° with the vertical, or a smash of your casting line will be risked. On the other hand, if the rod be kept too vertical an unfair tax is placed upon the strength of your middle joint. Another cardinal point, as every angler knows, is that you should never allow more line off your reel than you can avoid; that is to say, if your fish means running either up or down stream, and you feel instinctively that it would be neither prudent nor practicable to hold him too hard, then you must try to keep on terms with him by means of your own movements on the bank side; for it is to be presumed that, although you may have hooked your fish when wading in mid-stream, you have taken the earliest opportunity of wading ashore.

Keep nearly level with him, or down stream of him if you can, and get the weight of the water acting against him as well as the weight of the line. Never try to force a fish up a heavy stream unless such a course is absolutely necessary, for the weight of the water, added to that of the fish, may unduly strain your tackle.

That you may be compelled to try to prevent his going down stream at times goes without saying, for it may be absolutely necessary to do so; but to endeavour to force a fresh and strong fish up stream against his will is to court disaster. Should you have decided that your fish, if it is to be killed at all, must be kept in the pool in which he then is at all hazards, by judiciously giving him his head, by means of taking off the strain, may frequently induce him to abandon his attempt to force his way down stream, and, under the impression that he has already gained his freedom, he may often, of his own free will, head up stream once again. It is a risky, but often the only, course to adopt, if you cannot or will not follow a fish down.

Mr. Sidney Buxton, in that most charming of books, "Fishing and Shooting" (John Murray, 1902), sums up the whole matter admirably when he describes catching and playing salmon as "living moments."

I have seen stalwart soldiers, and I have one V.C. particularly before my eyes at the moment of writing, covered with perspiration and quivering in every limb after a long and successful duel with a clean-run fish. In this respect salmon fishing is ahead of trout fishing, for the contest is a more even one; though in my opinion the two, being distinct and incomparable, ought never to be put into the scales and weighed the one against the other.

Watch an old hand at the game, and observe how easily he controls the most determined and vigorous rushes of his worthy antagonist; take out your watch and see how long it will be before the 18 or 20 pounder is brought alongside for the gaff; and then watch the poor performer, hesitating and uncertain as to when pressure should be applied or licence given; see how long it takes him to land the 8 lb. or 10 lb. fish; count the number of times that he has to thank a beneficent providence that he has not lost him; and if, after so doing, you still incline to your statement that there is nothing in landing a fish, that the whole pleasurable excitement is concentrated in hooking him, then I can only reply that I don't agree. The contest between the hooked salmon and the fisherman is no uneven one—witness the number of hooked fish that escape—and it is one that is still capable of giving a thrill of real excitement to those who really love angling.

A salmon hooked from a boat in a large loch is, of course, a different matter; here the odds are so largely in favour of the rod holder as to unduly diminish the chances of escape to the fish. Such salmon fishing is outside the scope of our present argument, and falls into a totally different category. With river-bank fishing, and it is with that that we are dealing, it would be a bold fisherman indeed that would count a fish hooked as a fish landed, and a half-hearted angler that would be content to hand over to the gillie the cream of the contest between the fish and the man.

Apropos of this nervous excitement, in October, 1900, I formed one of a shooting party on Don side. The river Don ran within half a mile from the house, forming as perfect a series of natural pools as the heart of man could desire. My mouth watered when I saw it, and I longed to wet a line in it. I found, however, that my host not only loathed fishing, but was absolutely devoted to bridge. We had but short days out shooting, everyone rushing back to the lodge to get a rubber or two before dinner. Professing ignorance of bridge, I begged my host to let me try the river, as, having been lately fishing on the Dee, I had my rods and waders with me. With a pitying smile he told me that I could, of course, amuse myself as I thought best. With no loss of time I made my way down to the river side, and found it in grand ply. I was fully aware that the particular part of the Don that we were on was not popularly supposed to contain many fish at that time of the year, but it was well worth a trial, and I knew that a ship laden with lime had lately been sunk at the mouth of the Dee, and I fancied and hoped that some of the autumn fish might be finding their way into and up the Don. The pools were so perfect in shape that no gillie was needed to point me out the best rising-places; they spoke for themselves and told their own tale.

My first evening produced two clean-run fish

of 16½ lb. and 8 lb., and my host, when he saw them later, began to think that, after all, there might be something in angling. The second evening the river was up and unfishable, but by the third evening it had fined down into order, and I got a beauty of 20 lb. and a small salmon of 7½ lb. The glowing accounts I gave of the play of these fish at length excited my host, and, even at the cost of his rubber of bridge, the next evening saw him by my side, carefully fishing a leg of mutton pool near the house, where I had seen and risen a fish the night before. I had to hold the rod with him and show him how to cast, but I knew pretty well where my fish lay, and that he was within easy reach. We worked down to the spot, and, sure enough, up he came with a grand head and tail rise, hooking himself handsomely. Leaving the rod in my friend's hands, I told him that he had to do the rest. The first rush nearly pulled the rod down to the water level, my friend hanging on like grim death. Fortunately, the gut was sound and stood the strain. Nearly dying with laughter at his frantic appeals for help and advice, I shouted to him to keep his rod point up, thoroughly enjoying the fact that he was having a taste of what he had characterised as a "poor and tame kind of sport."

As I particularly wanted him to catch that fish I went to his assistance. Trembling with excitement and bathed in perspiration, he was, shortly afterwards, delightedly examining his first salmon, a clean-run hen fish of 16 lb. I never shall forget his shake of the hand and his exclamation, "By Jupiter! you have taught me something, this is worth living for!" Needless to say, he is now mad keen on salmon angling, and a very capable performer to boot.

Many of us, however, not quite so young as we were, are paying the penalty of imprudent wading in the times when we scorned to put on wading trousers. The rheumatic twinges, that hesitation about deep wading in rivers with bad bottoms, all these are largely bred of our former contempt for getting wet, and our ill-founded confidence in our powers of resisting the effects of such very minor matters as wet legs and feet. We therefore find our choice of fishing water still more limited: we seek fishings where many of the pools can be commanded from the bank side, or where, if wading be unavoidable, the bottom is sound and shelving, and where there are no round slippery stones to trip us up. Enough for most of us, if we are lucky enough to get into touch with a good fish, is it that we may have a longish travel over very rough ground, up and down, before we can call him ours.

One particularly bad-bottomed pool I remember very well in the Aberdeenshire Dee, not very far below Aboyne. It was a long pool, the head of water very heavy, the wading throughout simply vile. At the bottom of the pool was a big rock, nearly in mid-stream, and by that stone there generally lay

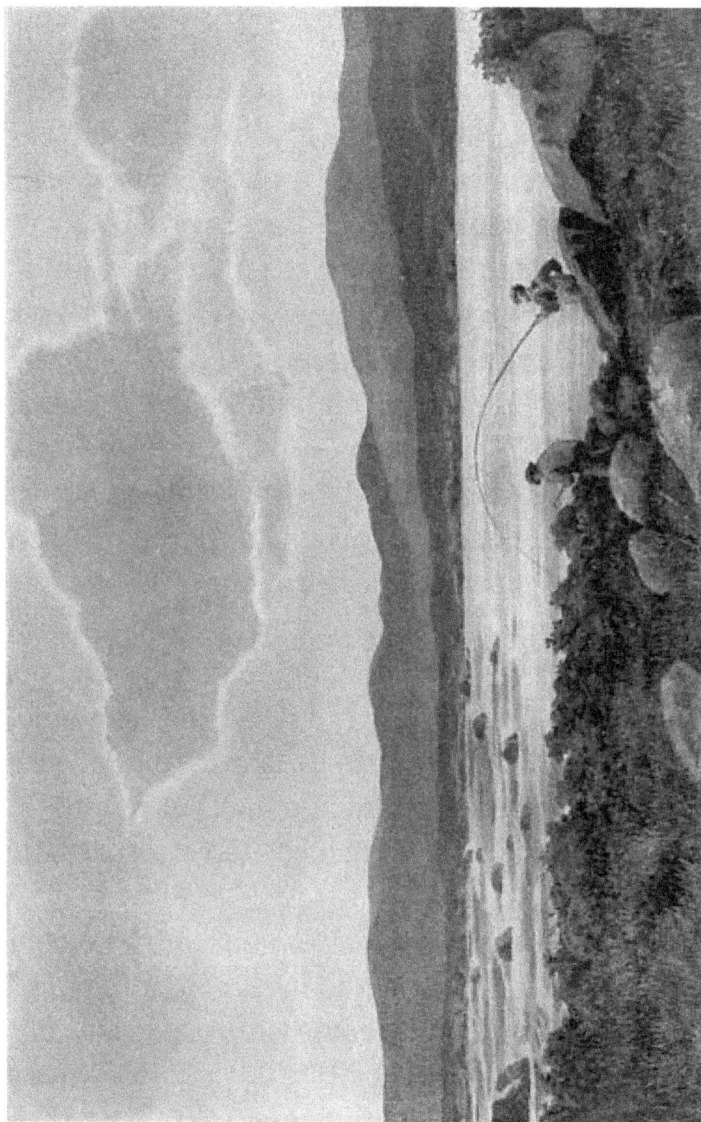

NEARING THE END

a good fish. To reach him you had to wade as deep as your waders would permit, your elbows almost in the water, leaning your body against the swirl of the stream, and taking cautious steps forward, inch by inch, to avoid being tripped up by the slippery big round stones. Then the best cast you were able to produce with your 18 ft. Castleconnel would just about reach him. I never could resist trying for him, though I knew he would go down stream if hooked, and it seemed impossible to follow him down, so I always half wished that he might not come. Wading back against that heavy stream, with a twenty or thirty pounder making tracks round the corner into the next pool, would have been no easy job; and, if you had succeeded in reaching terra firma, there were some big overhanging trees at the corner, beneath which the current had cut a deep hole. Mercifully for me, though I often tried for him, he never did take hold, though I rose him several times. It was always with a chastened spirit of thankfulness that I gave him up and went further down to try the easier waters of the Boat pool.

There is a local story of a mighty fish, hooked in that self-same spot, which took its captor down so that he was obliged, perforce, to swim the deep water under the trees, and was afterwards taken down, as hard as he could run, through pool after pool, until at length he managed to steady it in the third pool of the next fishing water. Then, after a period of sulks, during which both regained their wind, the fish ran right away up again to his old haunts, where he succeeded in getting rid of the hook against his favourite rock. All lost fish are big, and the lapse of time has not in any way diminished his fabled weight.

Perhaps the one drawback to salmon fishing as an art is that to which I have already alluded, viz., that the friendly stream corrects of itself all, or nearly all, errors of slovenly casting, and in that respect places the duffer more on a par with the really competent. On the other hand, knowledge and experience, and perhaps more particularly local experience, will assert itself in the long run, even against the adventitious success of the novice.

The mere fact of having really fished a pool, whether success reward your efforts or no, is of itself an element of enjoyment; the feeling that you have fished, and fished with a really working fly every inch of fishable water, is *per se* a cause of satisfaction and pleasure. Here you are master of the situation; on you depends your chance of sport, if any is to be obtained.

In grouse driving you may draw the worst butt; or, if you have the luck to draw the best, the birds may unaccountably take an unusual line, and, though you may have drawn the "King's butt," nearly every bird may pass over the heads of your comrades to the right and left of you. You are, as it were, a mere automaton, to shoot whatever may come within range; you may be the victim of circumstances, and may get very few chances.

In hunting, unless you hunt the hounds yourself, you have little chance of seeing, and none whatever of controlling, the best part of the game, the working of the hounds. Your main object is to be with them; they and the huntsman, or master, do the work, you are merely an accessory.

In fishing, whether it be for trout or salmon, everything from start to finish rests with yourself; you have to work out your own salvation; and I venture to assert that it is in consequence of this individual responsibility that fishing, apart from its other many merits, holds so high a place in all our affections.

I doubt whether there are many men who have not become aware, in playing salmon (and perhaps more often when the fish is nearly played out), of a second fish following the hooked one in all its movements and stratagems to free itself from the unwelcome attachment of the rod and line. It has several times happened to me personally, and on two occasions that I can call to mind I was within an ace of being able to gaff the free fish when bringing the exhausted and hooked fish past me for the gaffing process. I feel confident that, had I not been too much engaged in seeing that my hooked fish did not get free through any unintentional slackening of my line at that most critical moment, I could have done so successfully, so assiduous was the (apparently) hen fish in attendance upon the fish at the end of my line. Is this a mere matter of curiosity on his or her part, or may it be attributed to a feeling of *camaraderie* or friendship? I think no one can seriously contend for the latter hypothesis, as instances of affection between such cold-blooded animals as fish have never to my knowledge been even suggested. We must therefore, I take it, assume that it is mere curiosity, a desire to see why the hooked fish is acting so capriciously; and, if this be so, has it not a tendency to modify somewhat our views as to the necessity of resting pools after a fish has disturbed them by his being played? The following fish will, of course, have been taken out of the place where it would probably rise at a fly, and, therefore, out of any danger for the time being; but travelling fish are not infrequently hooked and landed.

My observations of salmon, such as they have been, have rather tended to inspire me with the belief that salmon, when resting in a pool, take little or no notice of what is going on round them. They will move just so far aside as to let a rampant fish pass them, gliding back into their former position the moment he has passed. How often, when fish are really "on the job," have fishermen caught their four, five, or even more fish out of one pool of very moderate dimensions, every square yard of which must have been disturbed by the vagaries of those caught before them? It seems to me that we are all inclined to be a bit too cautious and careful in this respect. When the water is in order, then I should be inclined to say, seize the happy moment, often short-lived enough, and don't waste time in going to other pools as long as you have any reason to suppose that the fish are "up," and that there are other occupants of the pool that you are fishing that may be grassed.

Somehow or other, if a fish be lightly hooked the information is conveyed through the line, as through a telephone, to the wielder of the rod. You obtain a kind of realisation that such is the case, no matter how well you have endeavoured to drive the barb home. And his subsequent play shows you how well-founded your feeling was. You are in constant expectation of seeing your rod point come up—unwelcome sight— and if you have the luck to get the gaff home, and the hook drops out of his mouth, you are not one whit astonished, only thankful that your luck for once was in the ascendant, and that you have not one more to add to the very considerable number of fish hooked and lost.

In the same way with a fish that "jiggers," I, rightly or wrongly, always set him down as being lightly hooked, and invariably offer up a thanksgiving if he be safely brought to bank. Can anyone tell us why a fish so acts? It is undoubtedly most disconcerting to the angler, and must assuredly have a tendency to wear the hold of the hook. But if it is so effectual, why do not more fish adopt it? Is it not permissible to think that my hypothesis is right, and that a lightly-hooked fish is able to appreciate that if he can only enlarge the hold of the fly he may get free? Or, if this is too much to attribute to fish intelligence, what other suggestion can be made? Of course, all my argument is upset if my premise is unsound, that it is lightly-hooked fish that employ the manœuvre of "jiggering" to free themselves.

The question is, of course, difficult of solution; at the same time, I have invariably found that it is just those fish that I have already set down in my mind as being lightly hooked that have resorted to that expedient.

I have always found it very advantageous to keep a good yard of free casting line in my left hand, letting this slack go at the end of the cast. This is exceedingly useful in getting out a long line; indeed, it has become such a part of my nature that I invariably do the same in dry-fly fishing for trout. In that case I find it helps me to pitch my fly more lightly, and to correct my length; it has one drawback in trout fishing, in that it prevents you from striking from the reel, but it does not inconvenience me, for I merely turn the wrist in striking a trout, so that the fact of my fingers gripping the line against the rod does not matter. It may not be quite orthodox, but I find it convenient, and always practise it; in fact, it is so much a matter of second nature with me that I could not give it up, even if I wished to do so. It is of great advantage, in fishing any pool, to have seen the river in all its various stages, so as to know as much as possible of its bed. As everyone knows, the places where fish rise vary as the river may be high or low; one place where, in high water, you might reckon on getting a rise if anywhere, would be absolutely unlikely when the river is low; and so also in the intermediate stages. Until you have become fully acquainted with the bed of the various pools, you are not in a position to make the best of them; that is why a gillie with local knowledge is so necessary. Perhaps you have fished a pool when it was in perfect order. The next time you try it the river has sunk a foot; it may still be fishable, but if you get a rise it will be almost certainly in a different spot from the time before.

On the Awe, in Argyleshire, a few years ago, after a summer drought the river had dwindled down to about half its normal volume. A rod had been fishing very sedulously a favourite pool of mine called Arroch. I watched him for some time, and at last suggested that I did not think he was at all likely to get a fish in the tail of the pool, where he was employing most of his energies. He replied that he had caught many a fish in that very part. I told him that it was doubtless true when the river was in proper order, but that it was most unlikely in its then condition. Somewhat nettled, he asked me to show him where I would propose to fish; and, having my rod with me, I commenced to fish at the very top of the pool, in a narrow, deep neck. At about my fourth or fifth cast with a very short line, I noticed below me the silvery glint of a fish that my fly had evidently moved. Stepping back a little, I began, with great deliberation, to fill and light a pipe, and then began again where I had originally commenced. At my fourth cast I saw the same glint, and also felt the fish, which had taken the fly when it was well sunk and was swirling about in the quick and heavy stream. It was, of course, a great piece of luck, yet it served to point my moral and adorn my tale. My friend was good enough to say that it was a revelation to him, that he would no more have thought of fishing that neck of the pool than of flying.

It is astonishing how many anglers are similarly constituted. They are content to fish a pool in just the same way, no matter what the state of the river may be. They never seem to fish from their heads, nor to bring any intelligence to bear. In a really big river it is possible to pick up an odd fish in the most extraordinary places. Once on the Carlogie water of the Dee, the river was in big flood, full of snow-brue, and apparently hopeless to fish; but the grilse had begun to run, and my time on the water was drawing to a close. Something must be done; it seemed foolish to stop at home and waste a day, so I walked up to the top of the Long Pool and fished my own bank down with a short line. My perseverance was rewarded, and I managed to secure three grilse. The great thing is to keep going, and to try to bring all your acquired experience to bear. A dry fly will never catch a salmon; your fly must be kept in the water, and not on the bank. The assiduous fisherman will beat the lazy one into fits.

National interest is, undoubtedly, being more constantly directed to the importance of our salmon fisheries. Thus, this very year, 1905, an influential deputation, headed by the Duke of Abercorn, was received at the Offices of the Board of Agriculture, the object being to obtain Governmental support to a private Bill that had been drafted with the idea of giving increased powers to the Central Board, and to boards of Conservators generally. The Bill, mild and tentative though it was in its provisions, met with but qualified support at headquarters, as it involved questions of finance, and possible rate aid to boards of Conservators in carrying out necessary improvements in cases where the local authorities refused to act. The question is, however, too vast and too important to be dealt with by piecemeal legislation of any kind, and, in regard to the vast national asset that is being squandered and frittered away, demands energetic legislation on a bold scale.

The salmon fishery industry is a factor in the prosperity of the nation, and the whole issue, with all its branches and ramifications, should be fairly and squarely tackled in a Government Bill, not in the interests of a class, but in that of the nation.

It is satisfactory to learn from Lord Onslow that the Government Bill dealing with obstructions and fish passes, though temporarily withdrawn last Session, still embodies the views of the present Administration. We must be thankful for small mercies, but this Bill merely touches one item of importance, and any Government that has the courage and wisdom to deal with the question as a whole will certainly have done something to merit the lasting gratitude of the whole country.

Since these lines were penned, the Election of January, 1906, has come and gone, and with it a vast change in the aspect of political matters. The point, however, that we are advocating is not a party question. It is a matter affecting the interests of all classes, and it is devoutly to be hoped that the new Government will take a "liberal" view of this important matter, and will bring forward a bill, in the interests of the nation at large, dealing with the whole question of our salmon harvest in the rivers as well as the sea.

GETTING THE GAFF READY

CHAPTER XV.
A TRIP TO IRELAND
~

Some years ago, when Ireland was greatly disturbed—it was the year after Lord Leitrim's assassination—a party of three, of which I formed one, decided to fish the Clady, in Co. Donegal. We went *viâ* Belfast and Letterkenny, bound for Gweedore. We had received many warnings against our projected trip, and were told that the "Boys" would not allow us to cross the mountains in our outside cars on our long drive from Letterkenny. Death's heads and crossbones, however, did not deter us, though our car drivers were sufficiently impressed and alarmed to insist that, if they took us, we should undertake to keep them at Gweedore until we returned. This we had to concede, and off we set.

The reports of the Clady were most temptingly satisfactory. The malcontents had burnt the nets at the mouth of the river at Dum-Dum, as they were the property of our landlord; the fish had, therefore, a clean run up the river. The talented author of "Three in Norway, by One of Them," had taken a fabulous number of salmon shortly before—report said fifty fish in one fortnight—so it was not likely that three sturdy fishermen would be frightened by paper threats. As a proper measure of protection we were each of us in possession of a revolver, more for show, should occasion arise, than because we were likely to need it for our protection. Our drive, if my memory serves me right, was over fifty miles in length, and was satisfactorily accomplished without any startling incident or need for the display of our lethal weapons. We were not sorry when it was over, and we were able to get off our cars and see what comforts the hotel could provide.

The local peasantry, of course, were not inimical to us as individuals, but were determined to score off our landlord, and to destroy or diminish his profits from the fishing. We had, therefore, to house and care for our gillies as well, in order to save them from maltreatment. Fortunately the river, though on the low side, was in fair order, and the pools were crammed full of fish—too full, indeed, for sport; and though we did not exactly equal the totals credited to our predecessor, still, we could not complain of the results. The fish, bright and clean, were not heavy—averaging not more than 10 lb. to 11 lb.—but they fought well. Neither were they by any means perfect in shape, being long and narrow, altogether less good-looking than their cousins of the Crolly, who use the same *embouchure*. These latter are perfect in contour and shape, more like Awe or Avon fish.

Sport throughout our fortnight's stay was distinctly good, though not remarkable, but the visit gave rise to some, to me, interesting experiences. Thus, in one pool, called the Pulpit pool, the usual cast is from the top of some very high rocks, as the name implies, into the cauldron below. The fish lie near the rocks on the pulpit side; from there the fly would never hang or fish properly; do what you would, it resembled a bunch of dead feathers. On the other hand, there was a convenient run on that side, down which a fish could be taken into the pool below; and, as the fish hooked there always would insist on going down, this point was one of some importance. On the opposite side of the pool there was a charming shelving beach, or bank, and if you could find a fly so well tempered as to stand being thrown against the rocks opposite to you, you were almost certain of a rise, as your fly then played admirably over the taking part of the pool. The problem was then how your fish could be played when hooked, for between you and the before-mentioned run was a line of serrated rocks, and a fish hooked that meant going down would inevitably cut you. He must, therefore, not be allowed to go down. Luckily, between you and this line of rocks was a deepish backwater, and this was our *deus ex machina*, and solved the difficulty. In this backwater we stationed the gillie, gaff in hand, and crouched down; no sooner was a fish hooked than, before he could realise the situation, he was unceremoniously hurried across the pool into the backwater, and there equally unceremoniously gaffed.

After two or three fish had been so treated our gillie remarked sadly, "Well, sorr, you may call this fishing, but I call it murther"; and so it really was.

As an example of how a difficulty may be overcome it was not without its value. The moral is that a fish, when first hooked and before he has realised what is happening, can be readily persuaded to act according to your will, as he will never consent to do later on. Just as a heavy trout lying amongst a bank of weeds can, if you can get his head up, be led holus-bolus over and across the weeds into reasonable water directly you have hooked him, so, in a similar manner, a salmon will often allow you a latitude in dealing with him at first that he won't give you a second time. Frequently the heaviest fish take some time after being hooked before they are roused to a sense of their position, and exert themselves to the full to get rid of the annoying restraint. The strong upward pull of a salmon rod, tending to pull him out of his natural element, is what a fish girds against, naturally enough, and I have frequently found it of advantage to take the strain entirely off a fish that is making too determined an effort to leave a pool. Give him his head and he will often stop his run and save you from the risk of being cut or broken. There is necessarily a considerable element of risk in so doing, but desperate cases often require desperate remedies. As with trout, so with salmon, hand lining can frequently be resorted to advantageously, and it is wonderful how easily salmon can be led by that means out of dangerous places, and even brought to the gaff; the strain being removed, they do not seem to resist an insidious and horizontal pull.

In the pool below the Pulpit I had my first experience in learning how to deal with a clean-run fish, hooked fairly and firmly in the thick part of the tail. I had, of course, had to play foul-hooked fish, but I had never hooked one in that part before. I was casting a longish line, and rose a fish at the tail of the pool. On my offering him the fly a second time he made a big splashy rise; I struck, and was in him. Down he went into the next pool like a mad thing. The travelling, for me, was bad, and the gillie had to steady me by holding on to the band of my Norfolk jacket. I held the fish as hard as I dared, but he was bent on running, out of one pool into and through the next; race as I would over the wet and slippery rocks, I never could get on terms with him, and he led me by some forty or fifty yards of line. As he had never shown so far and was playing so hard, both my gillie and I thought we were into a real big one. We were now nearing the falls above the sea pool; I was pretty near pumped out, so some resolute measures had to be taken. I accordingly, whilst holding on for all I was worth, sent the gillie ahead to stone him up. No sooner was he turned than he was done, and the gaff in him, and then only did we find out how he was hooked. He weighed no more than 14 lb., and had we known where the hook was, and had we not put him down as a real big fish, he would have never have been permitted to play such pranks and lead us such a dance. Had I held him really hard, his down-stream rush would soon have finished him, as the water running through his gills would have choked him.

One day we decided to try the Crolly, wishing to sample some of those beautiful fish, and, as it meant a seven-mile walk over the hills, we left our salmon rods at home, taking instead only double-handed trout rods. On arriving, we found the wind very foul, blowing partly across and partly up the river, so that it was no easy matter to command the pools at all properly with our small rods. One fish in particular annoyed us by showing constantly in a part of the water we could barely reach and could not command, so we instituted a kind of angling tournament, each of us in turn trying to get over him properly. Our gillies were watching intently and open-mouthed. One of them, Pat by name, had a peculiarly ugly mouth, with heavy, protruding lips; and whilst he was watching thus intently, the unkind wind brought my friend's fly, a big Jock Scott, right into his mouth, fixed it firmly into his lower lip, the forward cast sending it well home, and nearly dragging poor Pat into the river. We none of us felt equal to attacking the fly in its weird position, so we sent Pat down to the village, a mile or more away, to get the local doctor to extract it. Down he went, only to return an hour later with the fly still sticking in its former position, and having received a severe drubbing with shillelahs from the locals for having presumed to gillie for us. Pretty well black and blue all over, his lower lip enormously swollen, he looked indeed a sorry sight. Something had now to be done, so it then occurred to one of us to strip the fly, which fortunately was not an eyed one, and take it out the reverse way. This was done accordingly without delay, a plug of tobacco was stuffed into the gaping hole, a good jorum of "the craytur" was speedily administered, and Pat soon forgot all about his thrashing and his sore lip in his keenness to gaff the fish we managed to catch.

Owing to our being so severely boycotted, we had to manage for food at the hotel as best we could, and the monotonous diet of salmon in every form or shape, varied with a ham or piece of bacon, disagreed thoroughly with me, and somewhat marred the perfect enjoyment of my trip.

On Sundays we used to drive to the Protestant church in a big brake, so as to take the servants with us and protect them from possible violence; and one sermon we heard there amused us mightily. We were sitting in the big square pew just under the pulpit. The parson preached us an impassioned sermon on intolerance, and I must candidly admit that I have seldom listened to a more intolerant one. He launched forth into a tirade of abuse of most things, of absenteeism in particular, bewailing the sorrows of his poor, distressful country, and attributing the large majority of her troubles to a non-resident gentry. "They come here," said he, "not to do their duty or to help us, but merely to gratify their miserable sporting instincts" (and here we began to feel very small); "but," he added, leaning over the side of the pulpit in our direction, "not, gintlemen, that I allude to angling, for that is a grand sport. One of the greatest of the apostles, Saint Peter, was an ardent angler, and I am an angler myself." Mentally bowing our acknowledgments, we left the church, grateful that so eloquent a divine should be appreciative of our favourite sport.

One more anecdote and I have done. We were going back to England on the morrow, and were settling up generally, when my gillie Pat said to me, "Your honour, would ye buy me a pig?" "And why should I do that, Pat? Are you not content with your tip?" "Well, your honour, I don't want ye to pay altogither for it, but only to buy it for me." After some further conversation I consented to go up to the shanty on the hill where his old mother lived. There I found her haggling over the price of a sow; she averred that £3 was more than the sow was worth, the man was holding out for £3 10s. Eventually I became the purchaser at £3, and, paying the money, told Pat that as he had been a good gillie to me he could have the pig for his own. All the blessings of heaven were showered on my head by Pat and his mother; but no sooner had the dealer departed than Pat, producing an old stocking, extracted three sovereigns therefrom and solemnly handed them to me. Asked what all this comedy meant, Pat at once replied, "Ach, sorr, would ye have me let the praste know I'd got three sovereigns in my pocket?"

Were the nets at the mouth of the Clady and the Crolly kept within reasonable limits, few better rivers for summer angling could be found. Having seen their capabilities when the nets were perforce removed altogether, I gained an idea of what the sport might be in our sea-girt island, with its innumerable rivers, were the angling not throttled by the vast array of legalised nets that threaten to destroy, or at any rate reduce very heavily, the sport and profit of riparian owners.

That much has been done and that more is being done in this respect cannot be gainsaid. The allowance of longer slaps, the purchase outright of netting rights in individual cases, are undoubted steps in the right direction. But until the process is more universally applied its effect cannot be considerable. Salmon coast along such an extent of our shores before reaching their destination that bag and coast nets miles away may take heavy toll of the fish that are seeking your estuary, even though they would have a free run up your river if once they could attain it.

Is it too much to hope that some day a wise Government may take the matter in hand, not by piecemeal legislation, but with the determination of so apportioning and circumscribing the respective rights of all concerned and interested, that the price of salmon as an article of food may not be increased, and the true rights of both net fisherman and angler may be secured?

These two are so much bound up together that over net fishing must necessarily and improperly reduce the number of spawning fish, and thus injure the rivers which, by furnishing the spawning grounds, are the geese that lay the golden eggs. Kill the geese and you get no more eggs of gold. Treat the rivers unfairly, either by pollution or by over-netting, and not only will the net fishing industry suffer, but the general public also, for salmon will rise to famine price.

CHAPTER XVI.
SALMON AND FLIES

~

Why does a salmon take a salmon fly, and what does it represent to him? These are conundrums that are not readily answered. Obviously it cannot be because it represents any particular article of food to which salmon are accustomed when in the river. If one may presume to dogmatise at all upon so abstruse a question, it must be because their curiosity and predatory instincts are aroused by a queer object, moving with a series of jerks and a somewhat lifelike movement of fibres. Any salmon angler with the slightest experience will know what is meant by "hanging a fly" properly, and its taking powers as compared with a bunch of lifeless feathers floating down stream. So far we are all agreed; but when we attempt to discuss the details of the fly itself we are prone to differ amazingly.

Some years ago, on the occasion before alluded to, when I was fishing the River Clady, in Donegal, the nets having been removed for that year, the river was full of fresh-run fish—it was in July. There was a pool in which the fish lay in serried rows in the stream, which at that point ran under a steep, high bank. I lay down on the bank overlooking and a little behind the rows of salmon, and some twenty feet above them.

By shading my eyes I could make out all the fish as clearly as if I were looking at them in an aquarium. I arranged a code of signals with my fishing friend, and he went some thirty yards or so up the river to fish the pool. As soon as his fly began to work over the first line I signalled that he had got the length; there was, however, no movement among the fish. I then signalled to cast again with the same length of line. As the fly worked over the fish for the second time they all seemed to shun it, dropping down stream a foot or so, with the exception of one fish, which, separating from the others, came up some three feet to follow the fly, eventually leaving it and dropping back into his former position. A third passage of the fly produced similar results, the same fish moving again. He made a break in the water, which my friend saw, but he had come short. A fourth cast secured him.

I could come to no other conclusion but that the fish had been bored into taking that fly. His curiosity had been excited at first, and in ordinary circumstances the fisherman would have known nothing and passed on. Does not this tend to show that many a fish may be moved without our knowledge, and that a subsequent fly might secure him?

It is often thought that the first fly over a pool stands the best chance, provided, of course, that it is properly offered. Personally, I would just as soon follow a good angler down a pool as precede him.

Unless a fish breaks the water in his rise, the fisherman can tell little of what is happening below the water level, except when, by chance, a glimpse of a silver flash is accorded him. But he may have moved a fish with his fly, and, knowing nothing, will have moved a yard down stream, his next cast being a yard below the fish. The next fly, suitably offered, if it be about the same size, may lure our friend to his destruction. Could we all know exactly what is going on under the water out of our sight, many more fish would doubtless be brought to bank. Of course, on those days when the temperature of both air and water have attained that precise relative proportion that seems to cause a simultaneous rise of fish in every pool, the first fly will pay best, for on such happy occasions that fly, however ill delivered, may secure the best fish. And what fisherman cannot recall instances of "duffer's luck," the veriest tyro catching, perhaps, the fish of the season? I remember once trying to teach a would be angler how to cast, and in a most unlikely spot—the river being dead low—was endeavouring to instil into him the rhythm of the cast, and trying to make him get his line out well behind him. Holding the rod with him, I kept the same length of line, steadily flogging the water to the tune of "one, two," when, at about the ninth or tenth cast, a travelling fish seized our fly, and eventually came to the gaff, a clean-run salmon of 18 lb.

But surely the precise pattern of the fly, within limits, is of small moment; the size, coupled with the proper working of the fibres, is the main thing. Every angler has, naturally, his own favourite shibboleth, mainly, in my opinion, because he has succeeded with it, and therefore perseveres with it far more steadily than with any other pattern. In the same way local fetishes are set up, and when once adopted are hard to shift. On the Beauly, years ago, fishing on that lovely water in the spring, we were using the orthodox spring fly, a sort of exaggerated Alexandra, and were mainly catching kelts. When one of us suggested a Gordon (having lately used it on the Dee) the fishermen laughed us to scorn, and said we might as well fish with it on the high road. Nevertheless, the fly was tried, and nearly all the clean fish we got that week were secured by it. When our time was up our gillies begged for our worn specimens of the goodly Gordon, and the next lessee caught all his fish upon flies of that pattern; and, for aught I know, that fly may now be reckoned as one of the standard flies of the river.

To revert to the original query. Can it be answered satisfactorily? Surely it must represent some food taken whilst the salmon are in their sea home; and yet, if this be the only probable answer, how comes it that on some rivers, as is the case in Canada, salmon cannot be persuaded to rise at any fly of the kind? After all, whether the question is unanswerable or no, the glorious uncertainty of salmon fishing forms one of its most potent fascinations. If every bungling cast hooked a salmon, few people would care for the sport.

All this said, then, what form of fly are we to use? Here we get upon very debatable ground, and whatever conclusion we arrive at will probably be

HE MEANS GOING DOWN

strenuously opposed. The patterns of salmon flies are legion, many differing but slightly from others. Are we to credit salmon with such extraordinary intelligence as to believe them able to differentiate between varieties of almost similar flies, and to have such a correct eye for colour as to refuse a fly because the colour of the body or hackle is a shade unorthodox? The size of the fly, no doubt, is a most important factor, both as regards the size and volume of the river and the time of the year. It would be the height of absurdity to use in fine run water in the summer a three inch fly that would be a suitable lure on the brawling Thurso in the spring, and *vice versâ*. The finer the water the smaller the fly—within reason.

So far, I think, we are all agreed. It is when we attempt to reduce the vast number of flies now in vogue that differences of opinion will begin to assert themselves.

On the whole, perhaps, there will be less divergence of opinion about that singularly fortunate combination of fur, feather, and tinsel, termed the Jock Scott. It seems, to an extraordinary degree, to be effective on most rivers where the artificial fly is used. The combination of colour is most happy, and the fibres of its mixed wing give it, in the water, a most life-like appearance. Few anglers would care to be without Jock Scotts of sizes. Similarly, in bright water the Silver Doctor is a universal favourite, and justly so. As a direct contrast the Thunder and Lightning is bad to beat, and I should be sorry to be without a Blue Doctor.

Eagles, grey and yellow, hold their sway on the Dee, and the play of the feathers seems to be alluring in the quick waters of that river. How would such a fly suit the quiet waters of the Avon? You would imagine that you might as well fish with a mop-head! The fibres of Eagles require fast, fleet water to make them work, and to use an Eagle as your lure in slow-running rivers would appear to be most inappropriate. The play of the rod point may, however, be substituted for the play of the water, and a tempting opening and closing of fibrous and mixed winged flies can be obtained by a judicious rhythmical raising and lowering of your rod point. Indeed, if you watch an experienced salmon fisherman from a distance, you can tell at once the kind of water his fly is working through. If the stream be sufficiently broken and rapid to work his fly automatically, his rod point will be still. If the water should be sluggish, you will note the work of the rod top. It would, therefore, be folly to dogmatise on such a matter, and I should be sorry to attempt to do so.

Gordons, Butchers, Wilkinsons, and a host of others have their staunch advocates.

It is, however, unnecessary to run through the whole gamut; suffice it to say that in my opinion, a good selection of, say four or five, would be as effective as twenty or thirty. The main difficulty is local prejudice, and the uncertain kind of feeling—that if you had not discarded local favourites your blank day might have been fruitful. Once, however, you have shaken yourself free from this feeling, you will very soon gain full confidence in your theory. The blank day that you are mourning would probably have been equally blank if you had been equipped with all that local fancy could suggest. Can it be seriously suggested that salmon can be credited with sufficient intelligence to refuse a Silver Doctor or Silver Grey and to accept only a Wilkinson? Is it not rather that the fly that was accepted was presented in a most alluring manner, whilst the others which were rejected did not come within the salmon's ken in such a way as to tempt him? Are we not all too prone to change our flies on the slightest provocation, and are we not all inclined to have our own favourite fetish—a fly that succeeds with us simply because we give it ten chances to one of any other? The vagaries of salmon are universally admitted; at one time they will allow all lures to pass them unnoticed, and in the next half hour may take any fly, of the proper size, suitably offered. The relative temperatures of air and water have, I feel convinced, much to say with regard to this. The fly in which an angler believes, and with which, therefore, he perseveres most, will bring him more fish to bank than any other.

It goes without saying that the fly that is most in the water, in the fishable parts of the pools, of course, will catch most fish. The patient, persistent angler has that great advantage over his less energetic brother of the angle. What angler is there, who ties his own flies, who has not built up a combination of fur, feathers, and silk by the river side, and, on trying the novelty, perhaps after days of disappointment, has found it unexpectedly to succeed, and who has thereupon fondly imagined that he has found a "medicine," only to be equally disappointed the next time it is tried? Scrope, in his day, seems to have been satisfied with five patterns. To come to later times and later writers, Sir Edward Grey and Mr. Gathorne Hardy both advocate four only. The colour of the bottom of the river, of the sky, the brightness of the day, or its cloudiness, all these will affect our choice of fly, whilst the size and volume of the water will affect our choice of size.

CHAPTER XVII.
SALMON OF THE AWE

~

The River Awe, in Argyllshire, presents, to my mind, the perfection of angling water. A fine brawling stream, a constant succession of pools, some easy to fish, some only fishable by past masters, lovely, deep, roach-backed salmon trout—all these are bad to beat, and when one adds the fact that the run of the heavy fish takes place in June and July, after the Orchy fish have run through, the two months of all others, perhaps, when salmon fishing is enjoyable, I do not think any further arguments need be urged to enforce my point.

Were I a rich man—which I am not—I should feel inclined to do my best to secure the fishing rights on that merry little river in preference to many others of high repute. It is now many years since I first wetted a line on the Awe. My old gillie, Black Peter, or the "Otter," as he was frequently called, has, I fear, gaffed his last salmon and drunk his last glass of whisky, and (save the mark!) he was mighty good at both. I can see him now, in his somewhat tattered kilt, hanging on to the porch of the Clachan, trying to steady himself, to give me a right cordial welcome when I arrived. No more will he swim the Awe when in spate to land a fish for the "Colonel" that had jumped itself on the rocks on the opposite side of the river, some mile or two above the bridge—a foolhardy feat in such water; but he was always full of sport, and not infrequently, alas, equally full of whisky.

The head of water in this bonnie little river is always maintained fairly well by its being the affluent of Loch Awe. It is not, therefore, so liable to the quick rises and falls of most rivers. The loch is fed by the River Orchy, which flows into its north-eastern end, whilst the Awe, after passing through the Pass of Brander, forms its only outlet. All the Orchy fish, therefore, have to run up the Awe to get to their own waters. These fish run early in the spring, never dwelling for any length of time in the Awe; and, curiously enough, any tyro could at once differentiate between the salmon of the two rivers, though they have a common outlet to the sea. The Orchy fish are long, lanky, and plain as compared with the short, thick-set beauties of the Awe. I recollect once in Ireland coming across the same difference in fish using the same *embouchure*. It was in Donegal, where the Crolly and the Clady unite at Dum Drum. In this case also one lot of fish are poor in shape, whilst the others are of totally different calibre. And, moreover, in that case the fish never seem to lose their way. Seldom is a Crolly fish found in the Clady, or *vice versâ*. How accurate are the instincts of nature!

The lower reaches of the river Awe are very

varied and very beautiful. The river has churned its way through the solid rock. The two Otter Pools, Arroch and the Long Pool, are good examples of the rock-hewn gorges. In the latter, a fine quiet stretch of water, where local knowledge of the lie of fish is valuable, switching or spey casting is necessary if you wish to avoid being constantly hung up in the trees above. The Red Pool, just above the stepping stones, can only be fished from a plank staging fixed high above the water, and should you hook a heavy one at the tail end and he means going down you will be thankful enough when you have safely negotiated the return journey on the high plank and reached the shore. Even then you have plenty of excitement in store before you can hope to see him on the bank. The rocky sides of the chasm do not form a racing track. But get him once safely down to the Stepping Stone Pool and he should be yours.

This same pool, by the way, is not altogether the place for a beginner, for when the river is in order the aforesaid stepping stones have about two feet or more of fairly heavy water over them; and as they are well-worn boulders, somewhat inclined to be rounded on the top, and are placed at a rather inconvenient distance from one another, they are apt to make a nervous man think. One friend, I can well remember, when I asked him to fish the pool, absolutely declined, asking me if I took him for a "blooming acrobat." Below again we come to the Cruive Pool, a long cast from another staging, the fish lying on the far side, just about as far as an 18 ft. rod will get you. But be there in July when the sun is setting, the redder the better, behind the hills on the far side, and suddenly the silent oily water becomes broken with countless rises, also on the far side. Put on then a cast of sea trout flies and use your salmon rod, otherwise you will never reach them. Do not bother with a landing net, but run them ashore on the shelving bank below you and let your gillie take them off the hooks, and get to casting again as soon as you can. The rise, though a good one, lasts, I assure you, but a tantalisingly short time, and then the pool is as quiet and oily as ever, and you would feel inclined to stake your bottom dollar that there was not a sea trout within miles.

The Thunder and Lightning and the Blue Doctor are the local lures, and kill well. One year, when the river was low and the fish as stiff as pokers, I tied a "medicine" of my own that I fondly hoped would form a standard fly on that water, for its effect was admirable at that time. It was an olive fly, body olive silk ribbed with silver, tag a golden pheasant, dark olive hackles, a light mixed wing with golden pheasant topping. Having caught several fish that year with this fly, I got Messrs. Eaton and Deller to dress me a stock, and must candidly admit that never since then have I caught a single salmon with the "olives."

There are two pools, however, above the Long Pool that I have not attempted to describe—the lower one the Yellow Pool, an ideal, leg of mutton-shaped piece of water, where a beginner could not well go wrong, and above it the Bridge Pool, so called because the railway line crosses the neck of it. It was in this pool that I once had a rare bit of sport. The whole of the water I have attempted to describe was then hotel water, the fishermen staying at the inn having the right to fish for a nominal sum—5s. a day I think it was. But the river had been in fair order, and several good fish had been got. It was then rapidly getting on the small side. The records of the previous week having been published in the columns of the Field, the inevitable result was a rush of ardent anglers, and the dozen or so of good pools—nice water for two rods—was perfectly inadequate to accommodate the six keen fishermen who had arrived to try their luck. It was necessary, therefore, to "straw" for the pools, and to my lot fell the Bridge and Yellow Pools. The next morning, on reaching my little beat, I found the Yellow Pool far too low to be fishable, and there remained only the Bridge Pool. Fishing it down carefully twice produced no result, so I lit a pipe and clambered up on to the railway bridge to scan the water below me.

I was able, after a careful search with shaded eyes, to locate three fish, all low down on the far side, lying behind a big stone below the water and upon a slab. I could see at once that to reach them I should have to do my utmost in the casting way, and should have, moreover, to bring my line up through the centre arch of the bridge above me to get out the length I wanted; but it seemed to me that if I could get my fly to travel and work well over the oily water formed by the stone it ought to be irresistible to any well-conducted fish. So, putting on a small Thunder, I regained the water side. The second cast brought up the smallest of the three fish, who made no bones about it, but hooked himself handsomely, and was shortly after disposed of in the tail of the pool; he weighed a bare 9 lb. The other two I knew were better fish; one I had seen should be over 20 lb., the other, a very pale-coloured fish, I could not see distinctly enough to form any idea as to his weight. Back I went to my spying point, only just missing being caught on the narrow bridge by a passing train, to see, to my delight, that the other two fish were there, apparently undisturbed. After a few casts the fly went exactly as I could have wished, and there was the answering boil. "By Jove! that is the big one I think; anyway, he is hooked, and well hooked, too." After a long, splashy fight in the pool I got on terms with him, and he began to flounder, and then I could see I had the light-coloured fish on. The big one was still there, I hoped. The pale fish soon came to the gaff, and, getting it nicely home with the left hand, I hauled him on to the bank, a good fish, and in good condition, turning the scale at barely 17 lb.

By this time the pool had had a good doing, and I judged it advisable to give it a rest. The Yellow Pool, which I had fished down more for occupation than for anything else, yielding me no response—and, indeed, it was all I expected—I ate my luncheon, lit my pipe, and proceeded once more to my vantage spot. There, sure enough, was the big fish, undisturbed and immutable. Unable to restrain my impatience, I sent a fly (the same one that had accounted for the two other fish) on its errand of quest. But there was no movement, no reply, nor was there to two other changes of fly I put over him. Having nowhere else to fish, and being disinclined to try the Yellow Pool again, as I felt sure it would be hopeless, I sat me down to cogitate and look over my fly box. The day had become sultry and heavy, and clouds had been rolling up, and suddenly there broke a regular deluge of rain, turning the pool into a seething mass of big drops. Instinctively I ran for shelter under the bridge, but before I reached it changed my mind and determined to try once more for the big one in the heavy rainstorm.

Hastily putting on a Thunder and Lightning two sizes larger, I sent him out, braving the ducking I was undergoing. The first fly that reached the spot was answered by a fine head and tail rise, and I was fast in the big one. For a short time he played sulkily, either through not grasping the situation or through trying to induce me to believe him to be a small one. But I was not to be deluded, and, as he kept edging up into the big water coming down the centre arch of the railway bridge, I let him have a bit of the butt of my 18 ft. Castleconnell. But, with a savage shake of his head and strong whisk of his broad tail, he was now thoroughly aroused, and, despite all I could do, up he went, carefully threading the central arch and working up for all he was worth into the heavy water round the corner. My running line was thus against the buttress, but, despite the imminent danger of being cut, there was nothing to do but give him "beans." Fortunately for me my lucky star was in the ascendant. A convenient patch of moss between the courses of the bricks saved my line from the grinding process; the strain of my supple rod, combined with the weight of the water, did the trick. I felt him yield, reeled up as hard as I could, but, as he turned tail and came down (fortunately for me through the same arch), I soon had to give up reeling in in order to haul in the line by hand to keep touch with him in his downward rush. Steadying the line when he got ahead of me, I felt he was still on. Ten minutes of the fight against rod, water, and luck had been enough for him, and, rolling on his side, he swung round into the slack below me. I had had no chance till then of taking my gaff off my back; luckily it came off my shoulders quite freely, and the steel went home. As I hauled him out with some difficulty, the hook, which had worn a big hole, came out of his jaw; so my luck continued to the last. I could not make him scale 30 lb.; he was a good 29½ lb., and, inasmuch as I had never landed a fish of 30 lb. or upwards, that part was somewhat aggravating. But, as I toiled home that evening over the three miles of sleepers and rails to the inn with the three fish weighing just about half-a-hundredweight, I several times wished he had not been quite so heavy.

The upper waters of the Awe, above Awe Bridge, formerly retained by the Marquis of Breadalbane in his own hands, and therefore not open to the general public, can nowadays be fished from Dalmally Hotel. Through that nobleman's enterprise one of the two big cruives has been done away with, and there is to be an additional slap nightly, between 6 p.m. and 6 a.m. The results cannot but be both beneficial and prudent. The characteristics of these upper waters are totally distinct from those of the lower ones, being unusually broken and rapid, the pools small, and not easily distinguishable.

The pent up waters of Loch Awe, finding through the dark Pass of Brander their only outlet to the sea, take full advantage of their opportunity, and rush and boil over the boulder-bestrewn bed of the river in a way that renders it imperative that your gut should be of the best, your tackle sound, and your determination great that you will not consent to be a mere follower of a hooked fish, but intend to give him "beans" when necessary.

The Black and Seal Pools and Verie are fairly typical of the upper Awe waters; most of them are fished from planks rigged out on staging, and wading is not generally practicable. A hooked fish can never be reckoned on as caught, nor can you ever be certain of him until the gaff has gone home and your fish lies on the bank beside you. This remark, of course, applies in a greater or lesser degree to all salmon fishing; but here the perils from heavy water, combined with the rugged, rock-strewn bed, afford unusual chances of escape, and at the same time add much to the sporting charms of a successful capture.

CHAPTER XVIII.

Disappointing Days

~

Disappointing Days! How well we all know them, and how terribly frequent they are. Full of ardour and keen as mustard, we anticipate great things, only to find that another day of disappointment is to be added to the many already recorded in our angling diary. And it is sometimes so difficult to anticipate them; all the omens seem to be propitious, and yet the fates are inexorable.

There are days admittedly hopeless, when the river side is only sought for its companionship, and for the unknown possibilities of fortune; and others that are worse than hopeless, when to try to fish for salmon with a fly would be the height of absurdity, as, for instance, when the river is in high spate, or so full of snow brue or ice as to render your chances almost ridiculous. These, in a sense, are certainly disappointing; but it is not of them that I would write, but rather of those inexplicable days when all seems to be fairly propitious and yet we come home "blank."

Fortunately, fishermen are not easily browbeaten by unkind fortune, and these black letter days only serve to give a renewed zest to the future, in anticipation of the more fortunate days that we all confidently believe to be in store for us.

Everything seems on some occasions to go unaccountably wrong. The water may be in order, the fish up, and yet at the end of the day you have nothing but mishaps to record, your confident expectations have been rudely dissipated, and you have met with a series of misfortunes.

Perhaps on starting you find that you have left your flask or your tobacco pouch lying on your mantelpiece, and imprudently have turned back to secure them. That circumstance alone, in the eyes of your gillie, will prove amply sufficient to give you a "disappointing day." You have already discounted your luck, and must not grumble at the result. On reaching the water side you find that you have brought with you the wrong box of flies, and only have with you the one you had discarded overnight as containing those of a size too large. Well, you must make the best of it, mount the least objectionable of those at your disposal, and proceed to wade out into the stream with half your confidence gone. You soon realise that your waders, which had already given you warning indications of hard wear, are leaking somewhat unpleasantly. After working your way half down the pool you discover that your pipe is smoked out, and as you are in need of the consoling influence of tobacco, you propose to refill it, proceeding to knock out the ashes on the butt of your rod; in doing so the pipe slips through your fingers and disappears in the stream at your feet. It is impossible to recover it, so you are pipeless, and therefore inconsolable all day.

Some disappointments are sheer ill fortune; some we bring upon ourselves. You are, for example, casting mechanically, and therefore badly; moreover, you are not watching your fly, nevertheless you get a rise. You step back a yard or so, in order to be sure of getting the length right for the next cast, and in so doing forget the slimy green boulder that you had just negotiated on your way down. An awkward struggle, in which you have to use the butt of your rod as a stick to avoid an upset, does not serve to mend matters, but rather to unsteady you the more. At any rate, you have escaped a real ducking and are proportionately thankful.

Then, your mental balance being somewhat upset, you cast over your rising fish; he comes up well, a good boil, but you are too anxious and keen, and fairly pull the fly out of the fish's mouth. You have pricked him, and you will hardly get another rise out of him. Still there is a Will-o'-the-wisp kind of luck awaiting you, for near the tail of the pool you get a fair head-and-tail rise, and are fast in a good fish. He won't come up into your pool, but insists on making down, through the broken water, into the pool below. Having guided him to the best of your ability through the intricacies of the run, you hasten to get ashore to get on terms with him, keeping your rod point well up. More haste, less speed. The fact of your mental balance being upset reacts upon your bodily balance, and you catch the toe of your brogue on a submerged rock whilst working your way ashore, and this time you go a real "howler." Thoroughly wet, with a big chunk cut out of your wrist in your fall, you pick yourself up to find that you have broken your favourite rod point. Disconsolately you begin to reel up, the broken top meanwhile floating on your line in the water.

Still a gleam of luck: the fish is on, and, moreover, is complacently careering round the head of the new pool. Thoroughly aroused, you take the greatest care in getting on to terms with him again. Your rod has now a somewhat quaint appearance, like a dismasted yacht. Half the play of it is gone, and the top swirls about on the water in a most disconcerting manner. With set teeth, you grimly determine that, come what may, you will land that salmon. And you meet with some measure of reward, for after a somewhat prolonged duel, he begins to flop about on the surface, and to show unmistakable signs of having had enough of it.

With the greatest care you select the best spot for gaffing him, and successfully get the gaff free from your shoulder. Your now stiff and stodgy rod is, however, not best suited for bringing him in to the gaff. It is some little time before you get anything, like a fair chance. Then, with the rod in your left hand, your trusty gaff in the right, he is led in, down stream, and he flops about. The hold, alas, has been somewhat worn, and, just as you are making ready for your stroke, the fish makes one more roll and surge and is free. A wild scrape with the gaff only scores a scale or two from his side, and, slowly gliding out of sight into the deep water, he disappears for ever. You feel that you have only yourself to thank for such a *dénouement*, but that is scant consolation.

Damp and annoyed, you sit yourself down by the river side to try to make matters straight. Where is that waxed silk? At home, of course. So you have to content yourself with sacrificing a good length of the taper of your line in order to make a temporary splice. Taking all things into consideration, your efforts to rig up a jury top are reasonably successful, and it might yet kill a fish. If only you had a pipe to console yourself with, things might look brighter and better; but the loss of your pipe is an undeniably severe one. The pool that you are now fishing has a shelving stone bank on your side, the deep water being opposite to you. It is ideal water to fish, as the fly works out of the heavy stream into the shallowing water on your side. The wading, moreover, is easy, and the pool a long one, so that there is every probability of your being able to yet retrieve your fortunes, and of being able to account for a heavy fish before you have done with it.

Still keeping mounted the fly that, contrary to your expectations, had already deluded the former fish, you wade out and recommence operations. The cast, however, demands a certain length of line to cover the fish, and your rod is hardly the man it was; the breeze has increased a good deal, and is directly behind you; still, you manage to cover the water fairly well, and are beginning to get on better terms with yourself. A few yards down there is a good rise and a welcome heavy "rugg." The fly, however, comes away, and you are left lamenting. The long pool is steadily fished down, and some hundred yards or so lower you get another bold and confident rise. You strike, and the fly again comes back. Reeling up, sadly you wade ashore, and, on examining your fly, find the barb gone.

In all probability it was broken at the head of the pool on the shelving bank behind you, the strong wind at your back and the long cast with a weak rod having brought about the misfortune. Why, in the name of goodness, had you not examined the fly when it came back after your last rise? No doubt but that the barb had gone long before that. Mentally cursing your carelessness, objurgating Dame Fortune, and longing for the companionship of a pipe, there is nothing to be done but to mount another fly and to fish, albeit somewhat mechanically, the next stretch of water. But there is now no response. That inexplicable co-relation between the temperature of the air and the water that

THE FALL'S POOL

seems to cause salmon to rise has undergone some modification, the breeze has dropped, and the mists are beginning to rise. Do what you will, not a fish will move.

Had your luck been in the ascendant, or had you paid more respect to the superstitions of your attendant gillie, things might have been so different. You have had three good chances, each of which, under normal circumstances, might have been fairly expected to score, and that with flies that, in your judgment, were a size too large. Fate had determined that you were to have a "disappointing day," and you cannot say that you have not scored one.

In September, 1902, having received an invitation from an old friend to fish one of the upper beats of the Spean, I journeyed up North, full of eagerness. I had long wished to try that river. My host had informed me that that river was low, but that everything pointed to broken weather and rain; and though this forecast was true as regards some portions of Great Britain, the change never came during the fortnight that I spent on Spean side, that bonnie river getting finer and finer day by day, until at last it became a mere shadow of its former self. At the time of my arrival everything looked promising. Heavy clouds were gathering, and it looked as if the promised rainfall could not be long delayed. At the lodge I found, besides my host, another angler whom

I am also privileged to call an old friend, and in such company I knew that, whether sport were good or no, we should at least have a jolly time. That evening we discussed flies and angling details as only fishermen can, and with a last look out of the window at the murky sky, and a tap to my barometer as I turned in somewhat early, looking forward to the morrow with the keenest anticipation.

Early astir next morning, I drew up my blinds to find an almost cloudless sky and a bright sun. All the evening promise had been dissipated, and the rain-laden clouds had wandered out to sea to discharge their precious stores where least required. The river, though small, was, nevertheless, still fishable, and there were plenty of salmon up. At the lowest pool on the beat I put up my rod and fixed up the local "medicine"—a Thunder and Lightning—and, wading out, fished the pool down carefully, without result. My host then fished it, also blank. Several fish had shown at the tail, but we could not get a rise out of them. Then we wandered up the beat, trying all the likely pools in turn. In the mill pool I managed to get into a small salmon, about 7 lb. in weight, and duly got him out; otherwise our efforts were entirely unrewarded. It was a great thing to learn the pools, and to know where it was safe to wade, etc., and so I felt that the day was not a lost one as far as I was concerned, though of course less interesting to my friend S. and to my host. As we came home the clouds again began to gather, to lure us, Will-o'-the-wisp-like, on to further baseless hope, as the following bright, hot morning amply testified.

And so the days wore on, rocks gradually appearing where water had flowed before, shallows becoming stony strands, and the fish more pool-locked than ever. Finer grew the tackle used, smaller the flies. We were really learning the geography of the bed of the river to some weariness. After a few days S. gave up trying for the salmon, and contented himself with trout waders and a trout rod as being more productive of amusement. Being, however, of a more dogged temperament, I stuck to the salmon, fishing with the smallest flies I could get, and almost trout gut. By means of these allurements I did succeed in amusing myself, rising and hooking quite a respectable number of fish, but somehow or other I never could get a good hold of them; all were lightly hooked, and got off in playing or eventually broke me. One fish I was particularly annoyed with; he was a heavy one, well over 20 lb., and might have been 30 lb. I had often seen him showing in the pool at the end of the Red Bank. This formed really the head of the Mill Pool, but was now cut off from the main part of the Mill Pool by a daily lowering shallow some 1 ft. to 18 in. deep, through which sharp-cutting rocks jutted at intervals. In mid-stream quite a highish bank of stones was now disclosed, and on our side had quite cut off the flow of water and formed a large backwater. The pool was fishable with a short line, and the high, rocky bank behind formed a good shelter whilst working down the very rough bank side. About four o'clock one afternoon I saw my friend show twice in the head of the pool, and determined to give him another trial with the little Popham that had already risen fish. He took it grandly, with a head-and-tail rise, right up in the roughish water in the neck, and then proceeded to sail round the diminished proportions of the deep hole. He played very heavily, but did not jigger or show any signs of being lightly hooked. After some time of this kind of work, which was taking but little out of him, my light cast forbidding any heroic measures on my part, I began to wonder how I could manage to kill him. He could have got up into the pool above, where it would have been an easier matter to deal with him, but no arts of mine could induce him up stream. I thought that if I could get him down into the backwater I could more readily manage to play and kill him, so I walked him steadily down stream, and he followed for some distance like a lamb. Suddenly, however, he made up his mind for a run, or, realising the object of my manoeuvre, off he went, churning his way across the wide shallow, his back fin almost showing, bound for the main stream on the other side. Sixty yards of line were soon gone, then seventy, then eighty, and, as I could not follow, it was merely a question of when he would break me, when apparently he changed his mind, turned clean round and ran back through the shallow towards me for all he was worth. Holding the rod as high as I could to prevent my line being cut by the half-submerged, jagged rocks, and paying in line as hard as I could at the same time, I got him within twenty yards of the spot where he was hooked, the little Popham holding well, and with no slack line. Just as my gillie and I were congratulating ourselves that we had him now, up came the point of my rod, and he was gone. The light cast had been terribly frayed by his mad rush across the shallow water, and he retained my Popham and left me lamenting. It certainly was hard lines, when all the dangers of the run had been so successfully overcome and hooked fish were so scarce.

It is useless, however, to repine in such circumstances, and after all, in a very dead time, he had given me a good twenty minutes to half an hour of sport. My friend S. came up just as we parted company, and condoled with me. That same afternoon my host managed to land a 21 lb. fish on a stouter tackle, and he was not very red—the fish I mean, not my host!—although he must have been up some time.

The same thing went on all the next week. A few desultory showers did not help us much, and at the end of a fortnight's solid work I could only show two small salmon of 7 lb. apiece, my host one of 21 lb., and S., who had confined his attention to the trout after the first few days, had not landed any fish. And so it is—too often, alas!—that our hopes are doomed to disappointment. There were the fish, plenty of them; but also there were the gradually dwindling river and the expanding river bed. Nothing was wanting save a kindly and copious fall of rain—so much needed by three ardent anglers—rain that was falling only too copiously down South, whilst the normally wet North-West coast of Scotland was languishing for want of it.

A dear fishing friend of mine took a rod for February one year, and lived at Brawl Castle for the month at the rate of about £1 per day. During the whole month the river and even Loch More were ice-bound, and his rods reposed in the box. The trip must have cost him the best part of £100. So our Spean experience was as nothing to his.

And these disappointments make an admirable foil for those happy, though not too frequent, times when, for a wonder, river, fish, and weather are all we could desire them to be. How little we should value them were they of constant recurrence. So, consoling ourselves with these reflections, we enjoy to the full the pleasure of the company of kindred spirits, tie flies, grease lines, and fettle up rods generally, yarn away our fishermen's tales, drink nightly the toast of "Rain, and lots of it," and retire at night, confident, despite all, of the morrow.

Perchance your next holiday up North you may find your pet river in sullen, heavy flood, the skies pouring down upon the devoted hills a constant deluge. Each day you mark on the river bank the water level, only to find your mark submerged the next day. Supposing even it were to stop now. Could the river fine down sufficiently before the end of your stay to enable you to have a glimmering hope of a fish? It is possible, but doubtful. Next day's deluge settles the matter, and you are done. But still, it is a poor heart that never rejoices. Next time, after such a run of bad luck, you are bound to have an innings. Men who have the instincts of sportsmen and who deserve the name have a marvellous power of rising superior to adverse circumstances, and consequently get their reward, whilst the dead-hearted give it up as a bad job. Come good or bad luck, let your heart be in the right place. You will be able to extract from either much enjoyment and some experience, and will be just as keen to take the luck that comes the very next opportunity you get of testing it.

CHAPTER XIX.

SEA TROUT FISHING AND ITS CHANCES

~

For his size and weight there is no more sporting fish in the wide world than the sea trout. His play when hooked is so full of vivacity, so strenuous, you never know what he is going to do next. Half the time of the contest he spends out of the water in the air. He rushes hither and thither in the most unexpected manner, and having no particular stronghold or shelter to make for, such as his cousins, the brown trout, possess in their rivers, he tries by resourceful activity to rid himself of the irksome restraint of the rod and line. His rise, too, is so determined and so dashing—no quiet sucking down of a dun without much perceptible body movement, but rather a rapid dash to secure an article of food before his comrades can get it. Not much need to strike with him; he hooks himself pretty effectually by his own efforts. Given a single-handed split cane rod, fine tackle, and plenty of fresh run sea trout in a Highland river, and you have the prospect of as good a day's sport as any you ever enjoyed. You never know what the next cast will produce; it may be a half-pounder or something twelve times as big.

The worst of sea trout, from the angler's point

of view, is that they are rather gregarious and keep in shoals; they are always anxious to move up to the still deeps they love so well, and you may just miss the shoal—they may be just above your water. But if you do happen to hit them off, you will have no reason to regret it. Not many seasons ago I was invited by a friend to shoot with him on one of the many Western islands near Mull. Just before I reached the lodge, in my somewhat long drive up from the landing place, I met my friend, rod in hand, by a deep-looking, leg-of-mutton-shaped pool where his stream found its outlet into the brackish waters of the arm of the sea that looked like a land-locked loch.

"Get out of the trap; I've got a treat for you," were his first words of greeting; and then he explained that they had had, the evening before, the first run of the sea trout, and that, standing on a little rock in the brackish water, he had caught quantities of fine fish. Nothing loth to stretch my arms and legs, I took the proffered rod with many thanks, and fished the pool down carefully without a rise of any kind, or a sign of a fish. Putting on another fly, I tried it down again, and also the brackish water at its mouth, with similar results. My friend had foreborne to throw a fly on it until my arrival, and so he chaffed me unmercifully at my want of success after the extraordinary sport he had experienced the afternoon before. I told him that I did not believe there was a trout in the water, and as he had the netting rights, and had come down in the boat with the nets in it, we carefully netted the pool. My host was so convinced that the sea trout were there, that he offered to bet me any odds against a blank draw. He would, however, have lost had I taken his bet, for sure enough there was not a single fish in the whole pool. Whilst I made my way up to the lodge, he went up to try some of the higher pools, but not a rise did he get. The whole big run, shoal like, had run clean up into a small lochan, of which his stream was the outlet.

But when you happen to find them just in the right place, where you are, then you may congratulate yourself, if you have not too big a rod with you, for half the pleasure of angling is to suit your rod and tackle to the river and the fish. It is giving the show away and discounting half your sport to be "over-rodded." To fish, for instance, in the upper beats of, say, the Helmsdale, in Sutherland, with an 18 ft. rod is absurd. A 16 ft. or 14 ft. grilse rod will enable you to cover the water well, and the sport you will get from the 9 lb. to 14 lb. salmon in the well-stocked river will be greatly enhanced. A powerful 18 ft. Castleconnel will choke the fish unadvisedly. You might as well use a sledge hammer to crack an egg. So, too, with sea trout, a 14 ft. double-handed rod robs you of the better part of the sport and gives you no real satisfaction. On the other hand, if, as you may well do, you happen to get into a grilse or small salmon with your small rod and forty yards of line, then the sport you get will be worth living for, and will often recur to your remembrance in after times. You will need all your knowledge and resource not to be broken; you will in all probability have no gaff with you, and will have to tail him out, or, better still, persuade him to kick himself ashore on a shelving beach when played out. And it is extraordinary how little pressure of the rod is needed in such cases to keep his head the right way, and each kick and wriggle sends him further up the beach. Then getting between him and the river, having laid down your rod, you can put him out of his misery and despatch him.

A few seasons ago, when grouse shooting in the North, I was kindly given an opportunity to fish the Glentana beats of the Dee. The river was low, and as it was then early September, what fish were up were red and ugly, but a change to the river side was welcome, and I had never seen the pools in that part of the water. So, donning my waders, I took with me a 10 ft. 6 in. rod, cane-built, by Walbran, some light grilse and trout casts, and the smallest grilse flies I had by me. I also fortunately put in my bag a small box of Test flies. Nothing had been done for days in any of the Ballater waters, or indeed in any part of that brawling river Dee. The few anglers who had gone out had religiously kept to the orthodox salmon rod, salmon gut, and big flies, and had caught nothing.

When I got out of the dogcart and put up my little rod I noticed a smile upon the river keeper's face, but nothing daunted thereby, I followed him down the slopes to a beautiful pool below.

I put on a baby Jock Scott, and fished the pool most carefully. At the tail of the pool a big red fish gave a sullen kind of plunge, but not at my fly, for it was not near him at the time. I put the Jock Scott over him without result, and then tried him with a tiny Silver Doctor; but he ignored that also; and so I wandered down from pool to pool, learning a good deal of the river bed, owing to the lowness of the water. After a bit, I saw what I took to be the rise of a trout on the far side, so taking off my "Doctor," I opened my Test fly box and examined its contents. I hit off a gold-ribbed hare's ear, dressed on a 00 hook, which I thought might do, and wading out, had to make my little rod do all it could to reach the required spot. I fished the water above first, in order to soak my fly and make it sink. When I reached the place where I thought I had seen the rise, I fished with more care, and soon as my fly was working round below me, I felt a vigorous tug; something had taken it under water without showing. I was soon convinced that it was no trout that had laid hold, and got ashore as quickly as I could, but I had only forty yards of line and a little backing, so was soon compelled to take to the water again, as my fish was playing sullenly on the far side of the stream. I put on what pressure I dare in order to get on better terms with him, and this roused him a bit, for a vigorous run up to the head of the pool nearly ran my line out, although I was wading as deep as I dared do. My friend the keeper now became interested, and waded in alongside me.

Though big, the fish was rather craven-hearted, and I was soon able to get ashore again. However, his weight was great, and when he got into the stream down he went into the next pool, I following, rod point up and reel freely running. There were about forty minutes of this slow kind of play and several incursions into the water, and then I began to see my backing on the reel perilously diminishing. The 00 hook, however, still held well, and at last I had the satisfaction of seeing the big brute floundering on the surface. The keeper, meanwhile, had gone lip to the house to get a gaff, and, walking backwards from the river, I tried to drag the exhausted salmon within his reach; but, although the rod point was about level with the reel, the dead weight of the fish was more than I could manage. So my friend the keeper, deploring the irreparable damage that must have been done to my rod, waded in, thigh deep, and drove the steel into about as ugly and as red an old cock fish as I have ever seen. His under jaw was crooked, and he looked like an evil monster. He weighed just 17½ lb. As soon as the strain was off my Walbran rod it sprang up as straight and as limber as ever, to the great astonishment of the keeper, who had, oddly enough, never come across a rod of that description. Burying our red fish in the bracken, we went down a bit lower, and, two pools below the house, got out another cock fish of 10 lb., and returning home secured a third in the very same pool where I had caught the first; this proved to be a hen fish of 12 lb. They were all red and ugly, but the last one was, comparatively speaking, quite passable. As soon as she was gaffed we looked up the first fish; he had turned quite black, and was a gruesome sight. So, leaving the three fish with the keeper, to kipper or do what he liked with, I got into the dogcart and drove home. Of course, these fish would not have come to the gaff in the way they did had they been spring fish, or lately arrived in the water; but, all the circumstances being taken into account, the 21st September, 1900, will always recur to my mind as a real sporting day. Sundry other salmon has this little rod accounted for, and it is as true as steel and fit for any fight.

Such incidents as these add very materially to the interest of sea trout fishing, for, as I have said, you never can tell what your next cast may produce. It is small wonder, therefore, that good sea trout angling is so eagerly sought after and so hard to get. Your best chance of getting such sport is to go a bit further afield, to the Shetland Isles, the Orkneys, or somewhere a little out of the beaten track.

L'ENVOI

~

Seasons come and go, each in its turn bringing us nearer to the last, those that remain for our enjoyment growing steadily and inevitably fewer. But the instinct of sport, inbred in most of us, dies hard. I, too, would echo Mr. Sydney Buxton's words, and hope that when my time comes, and my loved rods hang useless in their cases, Old Charon will permit me to loiter awhile on the Styx, and cast one last fly on its dark and turgid waters.

www.ingramcontent.com/pod-product-compliance
Lightning Source LLC
Chambersburg PA
CBHW051825040426
42447CB00006B/376